100 Hikes in™

WASHINGTON'S
GLACIER PEAK REGION
3rd Edition

100 Hikes in™

WASHINGTON'S
GLACIER PEAK REGION
3rd Edition

Ira Spring and Harvey Manning

THE
MOUNTAINEERS

 Published by
The Mountaineers Books
1001 SW Klickitat Way, Suite 201
Seattle, WA 98134

© 1996 by Ira Spring and Harvey Manning

First edition 1985. Second edition 1988. Third edition: first printing 1996, second printing 1998

Published simultaneously in Great Britain by Cordee, 3a DeMontfort Street, Leicester, England, LE1 7HD

Manufactured in the United States of America

Edited by Dana Fos
Maps by Gray Mouse Graphics
All photographs by Ira Spring
Cover design by The Mountaineers Books
Book design and layout by Gray Mouse Graphics
Typography by The Mountaineers Books

Cover photograph: *Glacier Peak and trail to Green Mountain* (Photo by Bob & Ira Spring)
Frontispiece: *Lyman Lake and North Star Mountain, Hike 98*

Library of Congress Cataloging-in-Publication Data
Spring, Ira.
    100 hikes in Washington's Glacier Peak region / Ira Spring and Harvey
Manning. — 3rd ed.
        p.   cm.
    Updated ed. of: 100 hikes in Washington's North Cascades.
    Includes index.
    ISBN 0-89886-433-X
    1. Hiking—Washington (State)—Guidebooks.   2. Hiking—Cascade
Range—Guidebooks.   3. Washington (State)—Guidebooks.   4. Cascade
Range—Guidebooks.   I. Manning, Harvey.   II. Spring, Ira.   100 hikes in
Washington's North Cascades.   III. Title.
GV199.42.W2S663   1996
917.97—dc20   95–26759
                                                                   CIP

CONTENTS

Location

Status

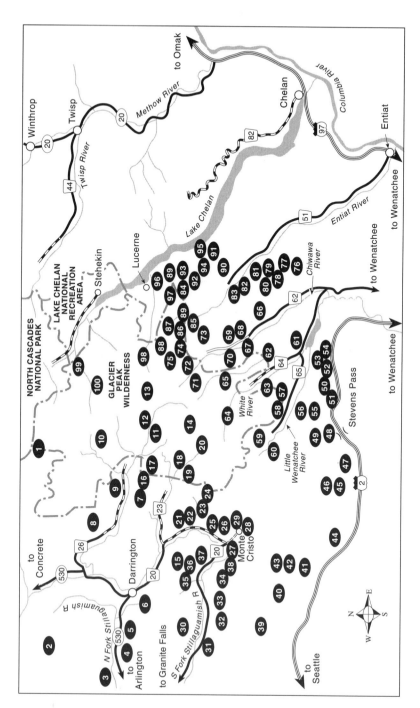

OF FEET, LOPPERS, SHOVELS, AND VOLUNTEERS, OR IF YOU CAN HIKE YOU CAN HELP

For years the forewords in the *100 Hikes in*™ series have focused on the injustice of converting some of our favorite foot trails into motorcycle speedways and giving maintenance priority to horse trails over those for feet. Considering their overwhelming numbers, hikers are still third-class citizens in the eyes of the Forest Service. However, conflicts are not the issue here, but the lack of money for trail maintenance that has become a major concern for all users. Hikers by no means should drop the motorcycle and horse issues. However, now is the time for them to exhibit their dedication, to mobilize their dominant number, by pitching in with volunteer labor to maintain trails.

Congress, for whatever reasons truly justified and purely political, has lumped the trail system with health care, pensions, and education and slashed and clobbered them all. Forest Service trail funding has been reduced to a third of what it was very recently.

Forest Service officials have no plans to "close trails." They say, "The real problem is that by deferring maintenance work a trail gets progressively worse and eventually deteriorates beyond maintenance and must be reconstructed. Or the trail is abandoned and the investment is written off." They estimate that many Cascade Range west-side trails, if not maintained, will disappear in three to seven years. And the way west-side greenery grows, many will be unpleasant to use after a single year not brushed out.

Reducing the trail budget has had some surprising and exciting results. Not only have volunteers responded in great numbers, helping mitigate the impact of the budget cuts, but they are generating a greater appreciation of trails. These volunteers will become our future trail and wilderness protectors. Washington Trails Association has taken the lead by organizing over 50 work projects in the summer of 1995 alone. Halfway through that season's program more than 6000 volunteer work hours had been logged, at least 12,000 hours expected by the end. Expectations are to double and triple the effort in following years.

Unfortunately, volunteers can be used only to do routine brushing and to clear drains and ditches; professionals are essential for using heavy machinery and undertaking major engineering, such as building bridges. Also, volunteers are efficient only on the first 3 to 4 miles of a route because any farther and they must spend too much travel time to and from the job, again; professionals are essential for long trails—but some districts have no funds to hire trail crews.

Glacier Peak from Kennedy Ridge, Hike 17

Trail crew volunteers on Pacific Crest Trail

Nevertheless, cutting back brush from the tread and keeping drainage ditches open are two of the major maintenance problems and are tasks that can be performed by anyone who can walk carrying a shovel or a lopper. Never go walking without tools. Carrying a lopper or a shovel is not practical for every hike, but hand clippers and even a small folding saw easily fit into a day pack.

Each hiker *who cares* must volunteer to at least two weekends a year. Yes, it is hard work, but comradeship grows as strangers on a trail crew team in the morning become great friends by the afternoon. Team spirit can make sweat and mud such fun that more and more hikers are getting hooked. To join a trail team, call Washington Trails Association's Trail Team Hotline, (206) 517-7032.

SAVING OUR TRAILS

Preservation Goals for the Year 2000 and Beyond

In the early 1960s The Mountaineers began publishing trail guides as another means of working "to preserve the natural beauty of Northwest America," through putting more feet on certain trails, in certain wildlands. We suffered no delusion that large numbers of boots improve trails or enhance wildness. However, we had learned to our rue that "you use it or lose it," that threatened areas could only be saved if they were more widely known and treasured. We were criticized in certain quarters for contributing to the deterioration of wilderness by publicizing it, and confessed the fault, but could only respond, "Which would you prefer? A hundred boots in virgin forest? Or that many snarling wheels in a clearcut?"

As the numbers of wilderness lovers have grown so large as to endanger the qualities they love, the rules of "walking light" and "camping no trace" must be the more faithfully observed. Yet the ultimate menace to natural beauty is not hikers, no matter how destructive their boots may be, nor even how polluting their millions of *Giardia* cysts, but doomsday, arriving on two or three or four or six or eight wheels, or on tractor treads, or on whirling wings—the total conquest of the land and water and sky by machinery.

Victories Past

Conceived in campfire conversations of the 1880s, Olympic National Park was established in 1938, the grandest accomplishment of our most conservation-minded president, Franklin D. Roosevelt. (Confined to a wheelchair and never himself able to know the trails with his own feet, FDR nevertheless saw the fallacy in the sneering definition of wilderness areas as "preserves for the aristocracy of the physically fit," knew the value of dreams that never could be personally attained.)

A renewal of the campaigns after World War II brought regionally, in 1960, the Glacier Peak Wilderness and nationally, in 1964, the Wilderness Act, whereby existing and future wildernesses were placed beyond the fickleness of bureaucracies, guarded by Congress and the president against thoughtless tampering.

Nineteen sixty-eight was the year of the North Cascades Act, achieving another vision of the nineteenth century, the North Cascades National Park, plus the Lake Chelan and Ross Lake National Recreation Areas, Pasayten Wilderness, and additions to the Glacier Peak Wilderness.

In 1976 the legions of citizens laboring at the grass roots, aided by the matching dedication of certain of their congress members and senators, obtained the Alpine Lakes Wilderness.

And in 1984 the same alliance, working at the top and at the bottom and all through the middle, all across the state, won the Washington Wilderness Act, encompassing more than 1,000,000 acres, including

13

the purview of this volume, two new wildernesses—Boulder River and Henry M. Jackson—and additions to the Glacier Peak Wilderness.

Is, therefore, the job done?

Goals Ahead

Absolutely not.

Had hikers been content with the victory of 1938 there never would have been those of 1960, 1968, 1976, and 1984. The American nation as a whole has a step or two yet to go before attaining that condition of flawless perfection where it fits seamlessly into the final mosaic of the Infinite Plan, and the same is true of the National Wilderness Preservation System. In the trail descriptions of this book we have expressed some of the prominent discontents with the 1984 Act.

There also are faults of omission from the newly created wildernesses: from the Boulder River Wilderness, Mt. Forgotten, Mt. Dickerman, Falls Creek and Peek-A-Boo Lake; from the Henry M. Jackson Wilderness,

Gothic Basin, Hike 26

West Cady Creek, lower Troublesome and Lake Creeks, Lake Isabel–Ragged Ridge, Gothic Basin, and Big Four Mountain.

The additions to the existing Glacier Peak Wilderness failed to include, on the west, Falls Lake–Otter Creek, Circle Peak, and the White Chuck River and, on the east, the lower Entiat River, the North Fork of the Entiat, Mad River, and Schaefer and Rock Creeks.

The above is only a very partial list of the remaining tasks.

It needs to be kept uppermost in mind that designation as "wilderness" or "national park" or "national recreation area" is a means, not the end. The goals ahead are not words on a document or lines on a map but the protection of the land these symbols may signify. Any other symbols that do the job are satisfactory. The *protection* is the thing.

In contrast to the immediate past, the preservationist agenda of the immediate future (that is, the coming several years) is focused less on redrawing maps than on employing any practical method to preserve roadless areas from further invasion by machinery. In fact, we are now at a stage where the saving of trails, important though that is, has a lower priority than the saving of fisheries and wildlife resources, scientific values, gene pools, and another contribution of wildland too long neglected, the provision of dependable and pure water for domestic and agricultural needs.

What in the World Happened to Us?

The wheel is more than the symbol. It is the fact. The National Wilderness Act so recognizes by banning "mechanized travel," including *but not limited* to motorized travel; bicycles—"mountain bikes"—are excluded too, for the simple reason that in appropriate terrain they readily can go 5 to 10 miles per hour, "unnatural" and often incompatible with the "natural" 1 to 3 miles per hour of the traveler on foot.

Outside the boundaries of dedicated wilderness, many trails can be amicably shared by bicycles and pedestrians, both capable of being quiet and minimally destructive and disruptive of the backcountry scene. Attach a motor to the wheels, however, and the route no longer deserves to be called a "trail"—it becomes a *road*.

In the past quarter-century conservationists have been busy saving Washington trails by creating a new national park and a bouquet of new wildernesses. Meanwhile, the U.S. Forest Service, without benefit of environmental impact statements, has been assiduously converting *true trails* (that is, paths suitable for speeds of perhaps up to 5 or so miles per hour, the pace of a horse) to *motorcycle roads* (that is, "trails" built to let off-road vehicles—ORVs—do 15 to 30 miles per hour).

In this quarter-century the concerted efforts of tens of thousands of conservationists have protected large expanses of wildland from invasion by machines—but during the same period a comparative handful of ORVers have taken away more miles of trails, converted them to de facto roads, than the conservationists have saved. As the score stands in 1995, only 45 percent of Washington trails are machine-free by being in national parks and wildernesses; of the other 55 percent, half are open to motorcycles—and thus are not truly trails at all.

When automobiles arrived in America the citizenry and government were quick to see they should not be permitted on sidewalks. The Forest Service (and let it be added, the Washington State Department of Natural Resources, or DNR) is slower to recognize that whenever there are more than a few scattered travelers of either kind the difference in speed and purpose between motorized wheels and muscle-powered feet is irreconcilable.

Thinking to serve the laudable purpose of supplying "a wide spectrum of recreational opportunities," the Forest Service initially tolerated ORVs, then began encouraging them, widening and straightening and smoothing "multiple-use trails" to permit higher speeds, thus increasing the number of motors and discouraging hikers, in the end creating "single-purpose ORV trails"—in a word, roads.

Federal funds were employed for the conversion of hiking trails to ORV use until that source dried up; since 1979 the Forest Service has relied heavily on money from the State of Washington's Interagency for Outdoor Recreation (IAC), using our gas tax dollars to convert trails.

Certainly, the Forest Service could not engage in such large-scale, long-term conversion of trails to roads if hikers were given the respect their numbers—overwhelming compared to the motorcyclists—deserve.

Threats to Wildernesses and National Parks

There have always been members of Congress who have threatened to "unlock" valuable resources. Members of the new Congress, with the support of big timber companies and Canadian and U.S. mining companies, are making an end run at decommissioning certain national parks and, in some cases, selling to the highest bidder. Could this be the fate of the Hoh River Rain Forest?

One can be certain that the same attempt will be made in wilderness areas such as the virgin forest along the White Chuck and Suiattle Rivers trails.

Hikers must watchdog Congress, either through environmental organizations or hiker-oriented clubs such as The Mountaineers or Washington Trails Association.

Hikers spoke up for the Washington Wilderness Act of 1984. By the many thousands they wrote letters to congress members and senators. The pen is mightier than the wheel, and it must be taken up again, by those same tens of thousands, to write letters to congress members and senators.

The Mountaineers
300 Third Avenue West
Seattle, Washington 98119

Washington Trails Association (WTA)
1305 Fourth Avenue, Room 518
Seattle, Washington 98101

INTRODUCTION

Broad, smooth, well-marked, heavily traveled, ranger-patrolled paths safe and simple for little kids and elderly folks with no mountain training or equipment, or even for monomaniacs dashing from Canada to Mexico. Mean and cruel and mysterious routes through evil brush, over fierce rivers, up shifty screes and moraines to treacherous glaciers and appalling cliffs where none but the skilled and doughty should dare, or perhaps the deranged. Flower strolls for an afternoon, heroic adventures for a week.

A storm side (the west) where precipitation is heavy, winter long, snows deep, glaciers large, peaks sharply sculptured, vegetation lush, and high-country hiking doesn't get comfortably underway until late July. A lee side, a rainshadow side (the east) where clouds are mostly empties, summer is long, vegetation sparse, ridges round and gentle, and meadows melt free of the white by late June.

Places as thronged as a city park on Labor Day, places as lonesome as the South Pole that Scott knew. Scenes that remind of the High Sierra, scenes that remind of Alaska.

In summary, to generalize about the North Cascades: To generalize about the North Cascades is foolish.

Rules, Regulations, and Permits

Except for blocks of state (Department of Natural Resources) land around Mount Pilchuck—Sultan River and scattered enclaves of private lands mostly dating from mining and homestead days, the entirety of the Glacier Peak section of the North Cascades is federally administered. The U.S. Forest Service is the principal trustee, responsibility shared by Mt. Baker–Snoqualmie and Wenatchee National Forests.

Most of the national forest lands are under "multiple-use" administration, with roads, with logging, mining, and other economic exploitation, and with motorcycles allowed on (too) many trails. Some areas, however, have statutory protection within the National Wilderness Preservation System, where the Wilderness Act of 1964 guarantees that "the earth and its community of life are untrammeled by man, where man himself is a visitor who does not remain." The Glacier Peak Wilderness was established in 1960. The Washington Wilderness Act of 1984 made additions to this wilderness and in the Glacier Peak area of the North Cascades established new ones: the Boulder River and the Henry M. Jackson. Within these, motorized travel is banned, as is any mechanized travel, such as "mountain bikes." Horse travel is carefully regulated, and though wilderness permits have been discontinued for hikers, they are subject to restrictions on party size and camping and must acquaint themselves with the travel regulations before setting out.

Maps

Each hike description in this book lists the appropriate topographic maps published by the U.S. Geological Survey. These can be purchased at map stores or mountaineering equipment shops or by writing the U.S. Geological Survey, Federal Center, Denver, Colorado 80225.

The national forests publish recreation maps that are quite accurate, up-to-date, and inexpensive. Forest Service maps may be obtained at ranger stations or by writing the following:

Mt. Baker–Snoqualmie National Forest
21905 64th Avenue West
Mountlake Terrace, Washington 98043

Wenatchee National Forest
P.O. Box 811
Wenatchee, Washington 98801

Neither maps nor guidebooks can keep up with all the constant changes by nature and man. When current information about a certain trail is sought, the hiker should visit or telephone the Forest Service ranger station listed in the text. Following are addresses and phone numbers:

Mount Baker Ranger Station
Sedro Woolley, Washington 98284
Phone (360) 856-5700

Darrington Ranger Station
Darrington, Washington 98241
Phone (360) 436-1155

Skykomish Ranger Station
Skykomish, Washington 98045
Phone (360) 677-2414

Lake Wenatchee Ranger Station
Star Route, Box 109
Leavenworth, Washington 98826
Phone (509) 763-3103 or 763-3211

Entiat Ranger Station
P.O. Box 476
Entiat, Washington 98822
Phone (509) 784-1511

Chelan Ranger Station
428 West Wooden Avenue
Chelan, Washington 98816
Phone (509) 682-2576

In the national forests a traveler not only must have a map published by the Forest Service but must have a *current* map. The problem is that the Forest Service has renumbered roads, made necessary when the number of roads grew so large as to require the use of more than three digits. For instance, a spur road from road No. 12 becomes road No. 1200830 and is perhaps shown as such on the new map, though the roadside sign may be simply "830." One ranger district is using parentheses, as (1200)830, another dashes, as 1200-830, and another commas, as 1200,830.

A traveler *must* know the right numbers because in many areas the Forest Service puts no names on signs, just numbers—the new ones. Your map, if it has the old numbers, will merely deepen your confusion. And we hate to mention it, but a few of the old signs remain, with the old numbers, so that even your *new* map compounds the difficulty. A word to the wise: Never leave civilization without a full tank of gas, survival rations, and instructions to family or friends on when to call out the Logging Road Search and Rescue Team.

Clothing and Equipment

Many trails described in this book can be walked easily and safely, at least along the lower portions, by any person capable of getting out of a car and onto his feet, and without any special equipment whatever.

To such people we can only say, "Welcome to walking—but beware!" Northwest mountain weather, especially on the ocean side of the ranges, is notoriously undependable. Cloudless morning skies can be followed by afternoon deluges of rain or fierce squalls of snow. Even without a storm a person can get mighty chilly on high ridges when—as often happens— a cold wind blows under a bright sun and pure blue sky.

No one should set out on a Cascade trail, unless for a brief stroll, lacking warm long pants, a wool (or the equivalent) shirt or sweater, and a windproof and rain-repellent parka, coat, or poncho. (All these in the rucksack, if not on the body, during the hot hours.) And on the feet—sturdy shoes or boots plus wool socks and an extra pair of socks in the rucksack.

As for that rucksack, it should also contain the Ten Essentials, found to be so by generations of members of The Mountaineers, often from sad experience:

1. Extra clothing—more than needed in good weather.
2. Extra food—enough so something is left over at the end of the trip.
3. Sunglasses—necessary for most alpine travel and indispensable on snow.
4. Knife—for first aid and emergency firebuilding (making kindling).
5. Firestarter—a candle or chemical fuel for starting a fire with wet wood.
6. First-aid kit.
7. Matches—in a waterproof container.
8. Flashlight—with extra bulb and batteries.
9. Map—be sure it's the right one for the trip.
10. Compass—be sure to know the declination, east or west.

Camping and Fires

Indiscriminate camping blights alpine meadows. A single small party may trample grass, flowers, and heather so badly they don't re-cover from the shock for years. If the same spot is used several or more times a summer, year after year, the greenery vanishes, replaced by bare dirt. The respectful traveler always aims to camp in the woods or in rocky morainal areas. These alternatives lacking, it is better to use a meadow site already bare, a sacrifice area—in technical terminology, "hardened"—rather than extend the destruction into virginal places nearby.

Particularly to be avoided are camps in soft meadows on the banks of streams and lakes (hard rock or bare-dirt or gravel sites may be quite all right). Delightful and scenic as waterside meadows are, their use may endanger the water purity, as well as the health of delicate plants. Further, no matter how "hard" the site may be, a camp on a viewpoint makes the beauty unavailable to other hikers who simply want to come and look, or eat lunch, and then go camp in the woods.

Carry a collapsible water container to minimize the trips to the water supply that beat down a path. (As a bonus, the container lets you camp high on a dry ridge, where the solitude and the views are.)

Carry a lightweight pair of camp shoes, less destructive to plants and soils than trail boots.

As the age of laissez-faire camping yields to the era of thoughtful management, different policies are being adopted in different places. For example, high-use spots may be designated "Day Use Only," forbidding camps. In others there is a blanket rule against camps within 100 feet (or 200 feet) of the water. However, in certain areas the rangers have inventoried existing camps, found 95 percent are within 100 feet of the water, and decided it is better to keep existing sites, where the vegetation long since has been gone, than to establish new "barrens" elsewhere. The rule in such places is "use established sites"; wilderness rangers on their rounds disestablish those sites judged unacceptable.

Few shelter cabins remain—most shown on maps aren't there anymore—so always carry a tent or tarp. *Never* ditch the sleeping area unless and until essential to avoid being flooded out—and afterward be sure to fill the ditches, carefully replacing any sod that may have been dug up.

Always carry a sleeping pad of some sort to keep your bag dry and your bones comfortable. *Do not* revert to the ancient bough bed of the frontier past.

The wood fire also is nearly obsolete in the high country. At best, dry firewood is hard to find at popular camps. What's left, the picturesque silver snags and logs, is part of the scenery, too valuable to be wasted cooking a pot of soup. It should be (but isn't quite, what with the survival of little hatchets and little folks who love to wield them) needless to say that green, living wood must never be cut; it doesn't burn anyway.

Both for reasons of convenience and conservation, the highland hiker should carry a lightweight stove for cooking (or he should not cook—though the food is cold, the inner man is hot) and depend on clothing and shelter (and sunset strolls) for evening warmth. The pleasures of a roaring blaze on a cold mountain night are indisputable, but a single party on a single night may use up ingredients of the scenery that were long decades in growing, dying, and silvering.

At remote backcountry camps, and in forests, fires perhaps may still be built with a clear conscience. Again, one should minimize impact by using only established fire pits and using only dead and down wood. When finished, be certain the fire is absolutely out—drown the coals and stir them with a stick and then drown the ashes until the smoking and steaming have stopped completely and a finger stuck in the slurry feels no heat. Embers can smoulder underground in dry duff for days, spreading gradually and burning out a wide pit—or kindling trees and starting a forest fire.

If you decide to build a fire, *do not make a new fire ring*—use an existing one. In popular areas patrolled by rangers, its existence means this is an approved, "established" or "designated" campsite. If a fire ring has been heaped over with rocks, it means the site has been disestablished.

Litter and Garbage and Sanitation

Ours is a wasteful, throwaway civilization—and something is going to have to be done about that soon. Meanwhile, it is bad wildland manners to leave litter for others to worry about. The rule among considerate hikers is: *If you can carry it in full, you can carry it out empty.*

Thanks to a steady improvement in manners over recent decades, and the posting of wilderness rangers who glory in the name of garbage-collectors, American trails are cleaner than they have been since Columbus landed. Every hiker should learn to be a happy collector.

On a day hike, take back to the road (and garbage can) every last orange peel and gum wrapper.

On an overnight or longer hike, burn all paper (if a fire is built) but carry back all unburnables, including cans, metal foil, plastic, glass, and papers that won't burn.

Don't bury garbage. If fresh, animals will dig it up and scatter the remnants. Burning before burying is no answer either. Tin cans take as long as 40 years to disintegrate completely; aluminum and glass last for centuries. Further, digging pits to bury junk disturbs the ground cover, and iron eventually leaches from buried cans and "rusts" springs and creeks.

Don't leave leftover food for the next travelers; they will have their own supplies and won't be tempted by "gifts" spoiled by time or chewed by animals.

Especially don't cache plastic tarps. Weathering quickly ruins the fabric, little creatures nibble, and the result is a useless, miserable mess.

Keep the water pure. Don't wash dishes in streams or lakes, loosing food particles and detergent. Haul buckets of water off to the woods or rocks, and wash and rinse there. Eliminate body wastes in places well removed from watercourses; first dig a shallow hole in the "biological disposer layer," then, if the surroundings are absolutely non-flammable, touch a match to the toilet paper (or better, use leaves), and finally cover the evidence. So managed, the wastes are consumed in a matter of days. Where privies are provided, use them.

Water

Hikers traditionally have drunk the water in wilderness in confidence, doing their utmost to avoid contaminating it so the next person also can safely drink. But there is no assurance your predecessor has been so careful.

No open water ever, nowadays, can be considered certainly safe for human consumption. Any reference in this book to "drinking water'" is not a guarantee. It is entirely up to the individual to judge the situation and decide whether to take a chance.

In the late 1970s a great epidemic of giardiasis began, caused by a vicious little parasite that spends part of its life cycle swimming free in water, part in the intestinal tract of beavers and other wildlife, dogs, and people. Actually, the "epidemic" was solely in the press; *Giardia* were first identified in the eighteenth century and are present in the public water systems of many cities of the world and many towns in America—including some in the foothills of the Cascades. Long before the "outbreak" of "beaver fever" there was the well-known malady, the "Boy Scout trots." This is not to make light of the disease; though most humans feel no ill effects (but become carriers), others have serious symptoms which include devastating diarrhea, and the treatment is nearly as unpleasant. The reason giardiasis has become "epidemic" is that there are more people in the backcountry—more people drinking water contaminated by animals—more people contaminating the water.

Whenever in doubt, boil the water 10 minutes. Keep in mind that Giardia can survive in water at or near freezing for weeks or months—a snow pond is not necessarily safe. Boiling is 100 percent effective against not only Giardia but the myriad other filthy little blighters that may upset your digestion or—as with some forms of hepatitis—destroy your liver.

If you cannot boil, use one of the several *iodine* treatments (chlorine compounds have been found untrustworthy in wildland circumstances), such as Potable Aqua or the more complicated method that employs iodine crystals. Rumor to the contrary, iodine treatments pose no threat to the health.

Be very wary of the filters sold in backpacking shops. The technology is steadily advancing and several products already offer some protection, but would you bet your liver on the claims of a marketing copywriter?

Party Size

One management technique used to minimize impact in popular areas is to limit the number of people in any one group to a dozen or fewer. Hikers with very large families (or outing groups) should check the rules when planning a trip.

Pets

The handwriting is on the wall for dog owners. Pets always have been forbidden on national park trails and now some parts of wildernesses are being closed. How fast the ban spreads will depend on the owners' sensitivity, training, acceptance of responsibility, and courtesy—and on the expressed wishes of non-owners.

Where pets are permitted, even a well-behaved dog can ruin someone else's trip. Some dogs noisily defend an ill-defined territory for their master, "guard" him on the trail, snitch enemy bacon, and are quite likely to defecate on the flat bit of ground the next hiker will want to sleep on.

For a long time to come there will be plenty of "empty" country for those who hunt upland game with dogs or who simply can't enjoy a family outing without ol' Rover. However, the family that wants to go where the crowds are must leave its best friend home.

Do not depend on friendly tolerance of wilderness neighbors. Some people are so harassed at home by loose dogs that a hound in the wilderness has the same effect on them as a motorcycle. They may holler at you and turn you in to the ranger.

Dogs belong to the same family as coyotes, and even if no wildlife is visible, a dog's presence is sensed by the small wild things into whose home it is intruding.

Theft

A quarter-century ago theft from a car left at the trailhead was rare. Not now. Equipment has become so fancy and expensive, so much worth stealing, and hikers so numerous, their throngs creating large assemblages of valuables, that theft is a growing problem. Not even wilderness camps are entirely safe; a single raider hitting an unguarded camp may easily carry off several sleeping bags, a couple of tents and assorted stoves, down booties, and freeze-dried strawberries—maybe $1000 worth of gear in one load! However, the professionals who do most of the stealing mainly concentrate on cars. Authorities are concerned but can't post guards at every trailhead.

Rangers have the following recommendations.

First and foremost, don't make crime profitable for the pros. If they break into a hundred cars and get nothing but moldy boots and tattered T shirts they'll give up. The best bet (but not a guarantee) is to own a second car—a "trailhead car"—arrive in a beat-up 1960s car with doors and windows that don't close and leave in it nothing of value. If you insist on driving a nice new car, at least don't have mag wheels, tape deck, and radio, and keep it empty of gear. Don't think locks help—pros can open your car door and trunk as fast with a picklock as you can with your key. Don't imagine you can hide anything from them—they know all the hiding spots. If the hike is part of an extended car trip, arrange to store your extra equipment at a nearby motel.

Be suspicious of anyone waiting at a trailhead. One of the tricks of the trade is to sit there with a pack as if waiting for a ride, watching new arrivals unpack—and hide their valuables—and maybe even striking up a conversation to determine how long the marks will be away.

The ultimate solution, of course, is for hikers to become as poor as they were in the olden days. No criminal would consider trailheads profitable if the loot consisted solely of shabby khaki war surplus.

Safety Considerations

The reason the Ten Essentials are advised is that hiking in the backcountry entails unavoidable risk that every hiker assumes and must be aware of and respect. The fact that a trail is described in this book is not a representation that it will be safe for you. Trails vary greatly in difficulty and in the degree of conditioning and agility one needs to enjoy them safely . On some hikes routes may have changed or conditions may have deteriorated since the descriptions were written. Also, trail conditions can change even from day to day, owing to weather and other factors. A trail that is safe on a dry day or for a highly conditioned, agile, properly equipped hiker may be completely unsafe for someone else or unsafe under adverse weather conditions.

You can minimize your risks on the trail by being knowledgable, prepared, and alert. There is not space in this book for a general treatise on safety in the mountains, but there are a number of good books and public courses on the subject and you should take advantage of them to increase your knowledge. Just as important, you should always be aware of your own limitations and of conditions existing when and where you are hiking. If conditions are dangerous, or if you are not prepared to deal with them safely, choose a different hike! It's better to have a wasted drive than to be the subject of a mountain rescue.

These warnings are not intended to scare you off the trails. Hundreds of thousands of people have safe and enjoyable hikes every year. However, one element of the beauty, freedom, and excitement of the wilderness is the presence of risks that do not confront us at home. When you hike you assume those risks. They can be met safely, but only if you exercise your own independent judgement and common sense.

Volunteers for Better Trails

For 10,000 years or so the only trails in the North Cascades were those beaten out by the feet of deer, elk, bear, coyotes, marmots, and the folks who had trekked on over from Asia. For some 50 years, starting in the late nineteenth century, the "dirty miners in search of shining gold" built and maintained hundreds of miles of trails, often wide and solid enough for packtrains. During the same period many a valley had a trapline, a trapper, and a trapper's trail, and many a ridge had a sheepherder's driveway. For 30-odd years, roughly from World War I to World War II, U.S. Forest Service rangers built trails to serve fire lookouts atop peaks and to give firefighting crews quick walking to blazes. In the late 1930s the trail system attained its maximum mileage and excellence.

Then the rangers began taking to airplanes and parachutes and the miners to helicopters and the trail system began to deteriorate. Eventually the Forest Service expanded the concept of multiple-use to encompass spending money on trails where recreation was the main or only use, instead of a subsidiary one as was formerly the case. Just about that time the United States fell on hard times and the funds for Forest Service—and Park Service—trails were largely diverted to maintaining troops in foreign nations.

Washington Trails Association (WTA) is part of the national trend toward construction and maintenance of trails by unpaid volunteers. The principle is simple. If each hiker spends several days a year working on a crew, trails can continue to be easily walked that otherwise would be abandoned by the government for lack of money. So, would you rather devote some days to whacking at slide alder with an ax or cutting through windfall with a saw, or would you rather devote tortured hours to hauling your pack through brush and crawling over logs?

For information on how your organization, or you as an individual, can join the WTA's effort, phone (206) 517-7032.

Protect This Land, Your Land

The Cascade country is large and rugged and wild—but it is also, and particularly in the scenic climaxes favored by hikers, a fragile country. If man is to blend into the ecosystem, rather than dominate and destroy, he must walk lightly, respectfully, always striving to make his passage through the wilderness invisible.

The public servants entrusted with administration of the region have a complex and difficult job and they desperately need the cooperation of every wildland traveler. Here, the authors would like to express their appreciation to these dedicated men and women for their advice on what trips to include in this book and for their detailed review of the text and maps. Thanks are due the Superintendent of North Cascades National Park, the Supervisors of the Mt. Baker–Snoqualmie and Wenatchee National Forests, and their district rangers and other staff members.

On behalf of the U.S. Forest Service and The Mountaineers, we invite Americans—and all citizens of Earth—to come and see and live in some of the world's finest wildlands and to vow henceforth to share in the task of preserving the trails and ridges, lakes and rivers, forests and flower gardens for future generations, our children and grandchildren, who will need the wilderness experience at least as much as we do, and probably more.

LEGEND

Symbol	Description	Symbol	Description
(2)	US highway	═══════	freeway or divided highway
(530)	state highway	▬▬▬▬▬	paved road
26	National Forest primary road	▬ ▬ ▬ ▬	gravel road
FH7	forest highway	══════	improved road (coarse gravel or dirt)
2040	secondary road (4 digits)	=========	primitive road (jeep road)
689	logging road (3 digits)	-----------	trail
790	trail number	++++++++	railroad
A	campground	....	cross-country route
⌂	backcountry campsite	· ▬ ▬ · ▬	boundary (national forest, national park, wilderness area, or recreation area)
▮	shelter		
⸙	ranger station		glacier
⬆	building or town		
⌂ or ⌂	fire lookout (tower or sitting on ground)		lake
) (	pass	⚘ ⚘ ⚘	marsh

25

MIDDLE AND SOUTH FORKS CASCADE RIVER

**Round trip to South Fork trail
 end 9 miles
Hiking time 4 hours
High point 2200 feet
Elevation gain 500 feet**

**Round trip to Spaulding Mine
 trail end 10 miles
Hiking time 6 hours
High point 3200 feet
Elevation gain 1500 feet**

**Hikable June through October
One day or backpack
Map: Green Trails No. 80 Cascade Pass
Current information: Ask at Mt. Baker Ranger Station about trail
 Nos. 767 and 769**

Standing on a high summit, looking out to horizons and down to valleys, expands the spirit. Standing in a low valley, looking up from forests to summits, gives humility. To know the North Cascades a person must walk low as well as high. The Middle Fork Cascade valley is one of the "great holes" of the range, an excellent place to learn respect. The companion South Fork is one of the grandest wilderness valleys in the range, giant trees rising high—but not so high as the giant, glaciered peaks all around. Expect brush, as these trails get very little maintenance.

Drive Highway 20 to Marblemount and continue east 16.5 miles on the Cascade River road. At the first switchback find the abandoned South Fork Cascade River road No. 1590; park here, elevation 1700 feet.

Walk the overgrown road. In about 1 mile is a difficult stream crossing. At 1½ miles is the start of South Cascade River trail No. 769, elevation 1800 feet.

The first ½ mile is up and down along the river bottom to a junction. The South Fork trail goes straight ahead, crosses the Middle Fork, climbs a bit, and enters Glacier Peak Wilderness. With modest ups and downs the way proceeds through magnificent forest to the end of

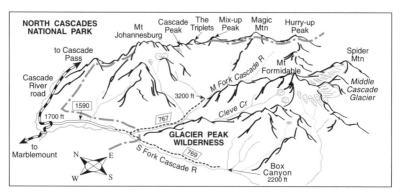

maintained trail at 3 miles from the road, at about 2200 feet. Good camps along the path. An extremely arduous climbers' route continues another 6 miles to Mertensia Pass, 5000 feet.

Back at the junction, the left fork, Spaulding Mine trail No. 767 (not normally maintained and thus very brushy), climbs steeply up along the Middle Fork as its cascades are falling down, sometimes seen and always heard. At the 2400-foot lip of the hanging valley the way gentles out in a superb stand of big trees. At 2 miles is a small creek; leave the trail here and walk several hundred feet down to the riverbank for a look up avalanche-swept Cleve Creek to a glacier on the west ridge of Mt. Formidable. Back on the trail, continue upstream in sometimes forest, sometimes avalanche greenery to the trail end somewhere around 3 miles, 3200 feet. By following gravel bars of the river upstream, or gravel washes of tributary torrents up the slopes of Johannesburg, enlarged views can be obtained of the Middle Cascade Glacier, cliffs of Formidable, and the summits of Magic, Hurry-up, and Spider. Camps abound along the river.

Middle Fork Cascade River crossing

2 FORGOTTEN TRAILS OF THE FINNEY CREEK AREA

Forty years ago, 100 square miles of roadless forest between Darrington and Concrete spread beneath the gaze of three fire lookouts and a lookout point, serviced by 80-odd miles of trail. Today that wildland has the look of a motheaten blanket. Clearcuts have chewed huge holes in the forest. Logging roads have obliterated 73 miles of trail. Of remaining trails, only the 4 miles to Higgins Mountain (Hike No. 3) and 1½ miles to Gee Point are maintained; trails to the other sites of vanished lookouts—Round Mountain, Finney Peak—have been abandoned where not destroyed. Nevertheless, despite the moth holes, the views are still great—of the horizons, if not the near vicinity. A determined, experienced hiker equipped with a 1960s map can locate these trails.

Round Mountain

Round trip 4 miles
Hiking time 4 hours
High point 5400 feet
Elevation gain 1900 feet
Hikable July through October
One day

Map: Green Trails No. 78 Darrington (trail not shown)
Current information: Ask at Darrington Ranger Station about trail No. 602

A charming Swiss-type view of mountains rising above farmlands in the Stillaguamish Valley. A trail was built here in the early 1930s but never a lookout building. Logging roads chopped the trail to a mere 2 miles and what remains has not been maintained for 30 years.

Drive Highway 530 to 5 miles west of Darrington and turn north on Swede Heaven Road (also signed 387th NE). Cross the river and follow road No. 18, then road No. 1850, to the unmarked trail. At first the way is an overgrown fire line, then an overgrown forest trail, and finally heather slopes.

Finney Peak

Round trip 5 miles
Hiking time 5 hours
High point 5083 feet
Elevation gain 1200 feet in, 200 feet out

Hikable July through October
One day
Maps: Green Trails No. 77 Oso and No. 78 Darrington

An imposing lookout site on a rocky ridge top. In 1970 only 4½ of 15 original miles of trail were intact. However, the Forest Service promised this remainder would be preserved. In 1975, only 2½ miles of trail survived. However, a promise was made that this stretch would not be shortened and would be maintained. In 1978 only 1 mile remained and the trail was abandoned. Promises, promises.

Hikers have had a tough time finding the correct road amid the maze of roads and logging debris. Once located, the tread is still good as it follows a thin ridge crest to the lookout site.

Whitehorse Mountain from Finney Peak

Drive Highway 20 to Concrete, cross the river, and follow the South Skagit road 8 miles. Turn right on Finney–Cumberland road No. 17. At 13 miles from the highway, go left on road No. 1735 for 7.5 miles to the road-end, elevation 4000 feet.

From the road-end trail No. 616 used to follow the ups and downs of the crest, the view's great. The trail was obliterated by loggers and never restored. Unless a miracle has happened, drive back 0.8 mile and walk road No. (1735)020 0.8 mile to its end and climb straight up the timbered hillside to intersect the original trail where it enters forest, drops under cliffs, and finally switchbacks very steeply to the 5083-foot peak.

The lookout was built in 1933 and burnt in 1965. All that remains is glass shards and rusty nails. The panoramic view is still there: saltwater shores, Olympic Mountains, Whitehorse, Glacier Peak, the Picket Range, Shuksan, Baker, and countless peaks between.

Gee Point

Round trip 3 miles
Hiking time 2 hours
High point 4974 feet
Elevation gain about 600 feet
Hikable July through October

One day
Map: Green Trails N. 77 Oso
Current information: Ask at Mt.
   Baker Ranger Station about
   trail No. 612

The lookout once perched on this rocky summit had views up the Skagit River to Marblemount and a 360-degree panorama of mountains. The trail now receives minimal maintenance. Drive Finney–Cumberland road No. 17 as described above, but go right on road No. 1720 and right again on No. 1722 to the end of maintained road. Hike the abandoned ¼ mile to the end and find a sketchy trail climbing through a clearcut to virgin forest and the wide tread of the original horse trail. In a scant mile reach its end at the remains of a storage shed. From here a footpath ascends up and around cliffs to the summit at 4974 feet. The lookout cabin was built in 1930 and burnt in 1964.

3

MOUNT HIGGINS

Round trip 8 miles
Hiking time 6 hours
High point 4849 feet
Elevation gain 3300 feet
Hikable late June to November

One day
Map: Green Trails No. 77 Oso
**Current information: Ask at Dar-
rington Ranger Station about
trail No. 640**

Seen from the bottom of the Stillaguamish valley, Mt. Higgins is an impressive sight, the rock strata steeply tilted, the dip slopes weathered clean enough to seem from a distance smooth enough to rollerskate or skateboard, very rapidly and finally. Seen from the top of Higgins, the horizons are equally remarkable. Located near the west edge of the Cascades, the mountain looks north, east, and south to peaks greater and icier than it is, and west to towns of the lowlands and islands in the Whulge (the original residents' word for "saltwater," or "the saltwater we know"). Just a stone's throw 4500 feet below are cornfields and pastures along the river. A person has the sensation of sitting on an overhang. This was virtually true of the fire-lookout cabin once located (and used from 1926 until 1949) atop a cliff on a 4849-foot promontory of the mountain.

Drive Highway 530 between Arlington and Darrington. Just 0.1 mile west of milepost 38, turn left on an obscure (the road is signed "SL-0-550," but the sign is hard to find), narrow Department of Natural Resources logging road—a poor place to be when the logging trucks are highballing. The old trail started right at the river, beginning with a ford nothing but horses ever enjoyed. This DNR road has obliterated the first 3 miles of trail; the good news, of course, is that it gets hikers across the river without risking their lives because in 0.5 mile a concrete bridge spans the Stillaguamish River. From there it climbs 2.8 miles to Mt. Higgins trail No. 640, elevation 1600 feet. In 1994 the trail sign was missing and the only clue was a wide spot in the road.

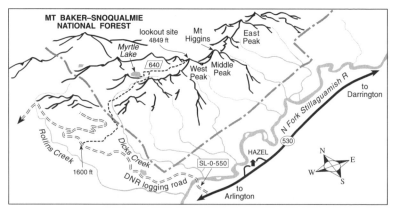

Mount Higgins from old lookout site

Some hikers continue up the road another 1.7 or 2.2 miles to bypass the first trail mile but the shortcuts are not recommended; they are poorly defined, steep, and lose a lot of elevation that must be regained.

The ascent from the official trailhead is very steep, on the order of 1200 feet a mile. The first mile has views from clearcuts (the tread in these is poorly defined). The way enters a deep-woods ravine. Neatly engraved on a high rock at about 2 miles is "S. Strom 8-1917," and on a corner of the rock, "K. Neste." Partly in dense forest, sometimes on rockslides, and for a bit through soggy meadow, at 3½ miles the trail reaches the lookout site and bursts out on the breathtaking view. (The summit of the mountain, 5142 feet, will attract only climbers seeking the undying glory that comes from signing a register book.)

About the names on the rock and the mountain: Walter Higgins homesteaded at Hazel, in the valley beneath the peak. Neste was an early settler-prospector. So was Sam Strom, a stubby and pugnacious Darrington Norwegian who acquired a lot of land. The Forest Service built a road on a Sauk Mountain tract Strom thought was his, so he put a gate on it and stood guard with his rifle.

4

BOULDER RIVER

Round trip 9 miles
Hiking time 3 hours
High point 1550 feet
Elevation gain 600 feet
Hikable almost all year
One day or backpack

Maps: Green Trails No. 77 Oso
and No. 109 Granite Falls
Current information: Ask at Dar-
rington Ranger Station about
trail No. 734

See for yourself the only long, lowland, virgin-forested valley left in the Mt. Baker–Snoqualmie National Forest. The Boulder River trail once was part of the Forest Service route over Tupso Pass and down Canyon Creek to the South Fork Stillaguamish road. It was also the shortest way to the fire lookout atop Three Fingers. However, when the Tupso Pass area was clearcut in the 1960s the trail between Boulder Ford and the pass was abandoned.

The walk is especially good in late spring when the high country is still buried in snow or in late fall when the maple trees have turned yellow. Views of mountains lacking, a cloudy day is as good as a sunny one.

Drive Highway 530 east from Arlington 19.8 miles (to just beyond milepost 41) and turn right on road No. 2010 toward French Creek Campground (sign may be missing). Drive past the campground and at

3.6 miles, where the road presently ends at a switchback, find the Boulder River trailhead, elevation 950 feet.

Trail No. 734 follows a long-abandoned railroad logging grade which ends in ¾ mile, at the edge of virgin forest (one can hear but not see Boulder Falls in the valley below). At 1¼ miles the way passes an unnamed double waterfall that plunges directly into the river—a favorite picnic spot. In ¼ mile is another lovely waterfall. With more ups than downs the trail proceeds along the valley, always in splendid forest and always within sound of the river, though it's mostly hidden in a deep canyon. At 4½ miles the trail ends abruptly in a campsite at Boulder Ford, elevation 1550 feet.

Boulder River Trail

Boulder River and unnamed falls

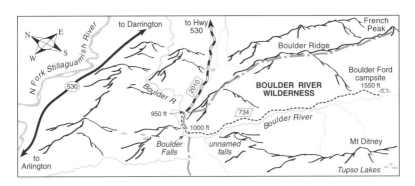

5 LONETREE PASS

Round trip 7 miles
Hiking time 7 hours
High point 4400 feet
Elevation gain 3650 feet
Hikable July through September
One day

Maps: Green Trails No. 78 Darrington and No. 110 Silverton
Current information: Ask at Darrington Ranger Station about trail No. 653

Built in the early 1900s by Mat Neiderprum as access to his limestone claims, this trail doesn't go anywhere near the top of Whitehorse Mountain. But it sure goes a long way up in the sky, to a little meadow with close views of a glacier and airplane-wing views to the Stillaguamish valley, where cows graze the green pastures and logging trucks rumble through the town of Darrington. Mr. Neiderprum expended minimum effort on such frivolities as switchbacks—his trail gains 3600 feet in 3½ miles. Maintenance is skimpy—some log-crawling and bushwhacking must be expected. And there is not much water. Many hikers prefer to do this in spring, going only to the first good views, turning back when snow grows deep.

Drive Highway 530 east from Arlington 24 miles. Where Swede Heaven Road goes left, turn right on Mine Road, passing several houses. Pavement ends in 0.5 mile. At 0.7 mile go left on forest road 2030. At 2 miles is the trailhead, signed "Neiderprum Trail No. 653." Elevation, 800 feet.

Though cruelly steep, the first mile is wide and smooth. In the second mile the tread is so-so (still steep). Then it becomes less a trail than a gully gouged by boots proceeding directly in the fall-line, but not always the same line; watch out for spur lines that dead-end. At about 3 miles additional entertainment begins to be provided by logs, mountain ash, huckleberry, salmonberry, and devils club.

At length the way enters a brushy meadow and follows a streambed, the first and last water. At roughly 3½ miles, 4400 feet, is a tilted

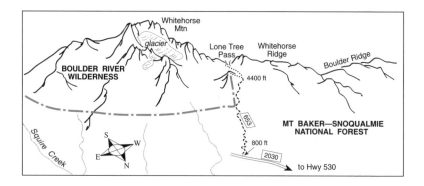

Whitehorse Mountain

meadow. The alert eye can spot flats excavated for Neiderprum's cabin and toolshed. To the left is a rocky knoll, a delightful place to nurse wounds and enjoy the view down to the pastoral valley, out to peaks of the North Cascades, and up to the summit icefield of Whitehorse. Hikers stop here. Climbers, properly equipped and trained, traverse steep snow slopes to the left and cross Lone Tree Pass.

6 SQUIRE CREEK PASS

Round trip 10 miles
Hiking time 6 hours
High point 4100 feet
Elevation gain 2300 feet
Hikable July through October
One day or backpack

Map: Green Trails No. 110
 Silverton
Current information: Ask at Dar-
 rington Ranger Station about
 trail No. 654 or 654B

Hike through lovely forest to a 4000-foot pass with a dramatic view of the seldom-seen cliffs of Whitehorse, Three Fingers, and Bullon—some of the steepest and grandest walls in the western reaches of the Cascades.

Three fingers (Mountain) from Squire Creek trail

Enter Darrington on Highway 530. Turn on Madison Avenue, then right on Squire Creek road No. 2040 (not signed in 1994). City pavement quickly yields to dirt. At 1.2 miles is a junction; go left. At 1.3 miles go right to the road-end at 5.5 miles. The trail-head elevation is about 1800 feet.

Pick up trail No. 654. The first mile traverses a lovely valley-bottom stand of virgin forest. The way then switchbacks steeply upward on rough tread. Whitehorse and Three Fingers tantalize through the trees until approximately 3 miles, at the foot of a huge boulder field, when views open wide and grow more dramatic with each step. At 4½ miles, 4000 feet, the pass is attained. Secluded campsites are scattered about the pretty meadows, but after the snowfields melt the water is chancy and dubious.

A shorter route to the pass—a steep, unmaintained, brushy 2-mile trail, No. 654B, gaining 2200 feet—misses the fine forest and has no exciting views along the way. From Darrington drive the Mountain Loop Highway 2.3 miles and turn right on road No. 2060. In 5 miles find the trail-head, elevation 1800 feet.

Squire Creek Pass

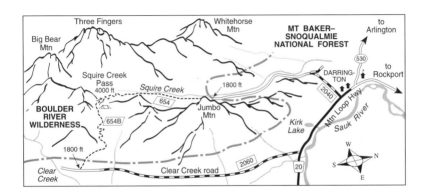

White Chuck Mountain from Circle Peak trail

SUIATTLE RIVER
Unprotected area

7   CIRCLE PEAK

Round trip 4 miles
Hiking time 3 hours
High point 5970 feet
Elevation gain 2100 feet
Hikable July to November
One day

Map: Green Trails No. 111 Sloan
  Peak
Current information: Ask at Dar-
  rington Ranger Station about
  . **trail No. 781**

In 1967 the lookout cabin was removed and the trail abandoned, but *presently* the path *partly* survives, through meadow flowers, blueberries, and heather to the circle of views from Circle Peak. "Presently" and "partly" are the key words: the vicinity is being clearcut as high as chain saws can operate without oxygen masks; 8 miles of trail have been obliterated. Due to major slides, the road may not always be open. The 1950 and 1960 forest maps show a second trail climbing from Crystal Creek to join the Circle Mountain trail near the ridge top. In the 1960s the trail from Crystal Creek on the White Chuck River side was destroyed by a clearcut and never restored. However, a trail of sorts has been established from the Crystal Lake trail (Hike 16) along the top of the clearcut.

Drive Highway 530 north from Darrington or south from Rockport to near the Sauk River bridge and turn off on Suiattle River road No. 26. In 10 miles turn right on road No. 25, over the Suiattle River. In just over 3 miles more go right again on road No. 2700. At 5 miles from the river road go left on road No. 2703 another 6.5 miles to the road-end, elevation 3800 feet.

From the road-end climb the edge of the clearcut to find Circle Peak trail No. 781 on the hillside about 150 feet above the road. For most of the way the trail is in decent shape, a testimony to the absence of horses and motorcycles. Nature has been kind, too; surprisingly few logs must be crawled over and only in a few spots has the tread slid out. At about ⅓ mile is a stream, in the first meadow. A long ½ mile more attains the second meadow. At a long 1 mile the way switchbacks up a large meadow where the tread may be hard to find amid the hellebore, aster, bistort, valerian, and other good and bright things. At 1¾ miles the route tops a 5600-foot ridge.

A way trail to a spring used by the lookout switchbacks 200 feet down toward Indigo Lake, ending on top of a cliff some 600 feet above the lake. Stay on the main trail contouring the east slope of the ridge, climbing from a heather meadow to a flower-speckled rock ridge crest and the end of the lookout trail, 5970 feet, 2 miles from the road. Let the eyes swing the circle of peaks—Pugh, White Chuck, Sloan, Green, Huckleberry, and, dominating all, Glacier Peak.

The lookout site isn't far away but is a rock scramble, not recommended for a hiker, and anyhow the 5983-foot summit has little more to offer.

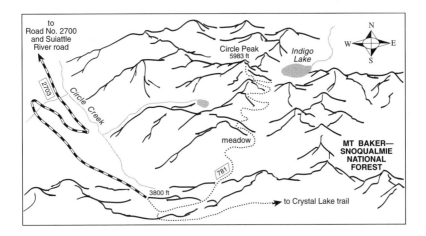

8 HUCKLEBERRY MOUNTAIN

Round trip to viewpoint 13 miles
Hiking time 9 hours
High point 5483 feet
Elevation gain 4500 feet
Hikable July through September
One day or backpack

Map: Green Trails No. 79
  Snowking
Current information: Ask at Dar-
  rington Ranger Station about
  trail No. 780

Most one-time lookout trails of the Cascades have long since had their bottoms amputated by logging trucks, and many their midsections as well, and some have been just about scalped. Clearcuts have climbed so close to timberline that hikers often pass through only the uppermost forest zones. This trail—gloryosky—has survived intact all the way from the valley to the sky. The lower stories are a virgin forest of tall, old Douglas fir and western hemlock, the middle stories are in the zones of silver fir and mountain hemlock, equally virgin, and the top stories are pristine parklands and subalpine meadows wide open to all-around views of craggy peaks and glowing glaciers. Rejoice in the bottom-to-top display of forests of the Cascade west slope. However, don't expect to pack the whole experience into a quick afternoon. Indeed, only the best-oiled hiking machines will find the trip practical for a day, and it's a long huffer-puffer with overnight packs.

Drive Suiattle River road No. 26 (Hike 7) 14.5 miles and find a small parking place a few feet beyond Huckleberry Mountain trail No. 780, elevation 1000 feet.

The well-graded, well-maintained trail gains 800 feet a mile, an ideal steepness for a hiker. The forest shadows minimize sweat and many streams are passed. At 3¾ miles is Fred Bugner Camp, about 3800 feet, with plenty of water all summer. In about 1 mile, at about 4800 feet, is another campsite with enough water, usually—and probably the last.

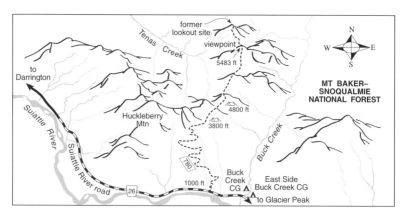

White Chuck Mountain from Huckleberry Mountain

At about 5 miles the grade slackens, even drops a bit, contouring below a ridge crest. Views commence, dominated by the spectacular north
face of White Chuck Mountain. At 5½ miles, about 5000 feet, the trail
contours a steep slope. At 6½ miles the trail climbs into meadows, to a
5483-foot high point, and enough views to satisfy a hog. Down to the
west are the logging roads of Tenas Creek; to the east, the preserved forests of Buck Creek. Across the deep valley are the emerald slopes of
Green Mountain, the rocky-snowy cirques of Buckindy and Snowking,
and the Pleistocene grandeur of the Glacier Peak Wilderness.

The site of the old lookout is close and the slopes to it invitingly
meadowy. To get there, however, the tread is faint and drops 400 feet
from the viewpoint and then climbs 800. A party must begin thinking
in terms of a 3-day or 4-day trip, backpacking a gallon of water per person to supply a dry Camp Two.

9 GREEN MOUNTAIN

Round trip 8 miles
Hiking time 6 hours
High point 6500 feet
Elevation gain 3100 feet
Hikable late June through
October

One day or backpack
Map: Green Trails No. 80 Cascade
Pass
Current information: Ask at Dar-
rington Ranger Station about
trail No. 782

The name of the peak may seem banal, but few people have ever looked up to it from the Suiattle River valley without exclaiming, "What a *green* mountain!" The trail climbs through these remarkable meadows to a lookout summit with magnificent views to every point of the compass.

Drive Suiattle River road No. 26 (Hike 7) almost 19 miles to Green Mountain road No. 2680. Turn left and drive 6 miles to the road-end in a logging patch, elevation about 3400 feet. Find the trail sign above the road several hundred yards before the road-end.

The trail climbs a rather steep mile in mossy forest to a grubby hunters' camp with a year-round spring, then enters the vast meadow system admired from below. First are fields of bracken fern and subalpine plants, then, on higher switchbacks, a feast (in season) of blueberries. Views begin—down to Suiattle forests and out to White Chuck Mountain and Glacier Peak. More meadows, and views of Mt. Pugh and Sloan Peak beyond the intervening ridge of Lime Mountain.

At 2 miles, 5200 feet, the trail rounds a shoulder and in ½ mile

Pipsissewa

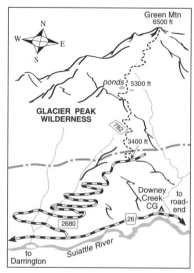

traverses and drops 100 feet to a pair of shallow ponds amid gardens. Pleasant camps here, and all-summer water; please use established sites away from the ponds. Wood is scarce, so carry a stove. No camping allowed beyond here.

A short way above the pond basin the trail enters a larger, wide-open basin. Please stay on the trail. The Forest Service is trying to restore the vegetation in erosion channels caused by hasty-footed hikers cutting switchbacks. The summit can now be seen directly above, and also Glacier Peak. Climb in flowers to the ridge and along the crest to the 6500-foot summit, 4 miles.

Look north along the ridge to the nearby cliffs and glaciers of 7311-foot Buckindy. Look up Downey Creek to peaks of the Ptarmigan Traverse from Dome north to Formidable. Look up Milk Creek to the Ptarmigan Glacier on Glacier Peak. Look in all directions to other peaks, too many to name.

Glacier Peak from Green Mountain

10 DOWNEY CREEK– BACHELOR MEADOWS

Round trip 23½ miles
Allow 2–3 days
High point 5900 feet
Elevation gain 4500 feet
Hikable mid-July through
September

Map: Green Trails No. 80 Cascade
Pass (partly)
Current information: Ask at Dar-
rington Ranger Station about
trail Nos. 768 and 796

A pleasant hike through virgin forest along Downey Creek to Sixmile Camp. For those with the energy and ambition, and experience in traveling rough wilderness, it's a tough climb some 5½ miles farther to meadows under 8264-foot Spire Point, with views of deep and blue Cub and Itswoot Lakes, Dome Peak, Glacier Peak, and other icy mountains. Downey Creek trail gets very little maintenance, Bachelor Creek none.

Drive Suiattle River road No. 26 (Hike 7) 21 miles (a bit past Downey Creek Campground) and find the Downey Creek trailhead, elevation 1450 feet.

The first mile climbs steadily, then the way levels into easy ups and downs amid tall firs, hemlocks, and cedars, crossing small streams, sometimes coming close to the river. At 6¼ miles, 2400 feet, is Sixmile Camp.

For Bachelor Meadows, proceed onward and now upward alongside Bachelor Creek, initially on well-graded trail which is no longer maintained. At 7 miles the way becomes a route trampled out by boots, climbing over roots and plunging through gooey bogs. The windfalls have not been cut and other problems abound. In about 2 miles cross Bachelor Creek. The track becomes even harder to follow through a boulder-strewn meadow deep in alders and willows. Spire Point comes into view. At about 3½ miles good campsites commence; choose one under trees, away from fragile heather.

Now the way climbs a short but steep mile and at 5400 feet abruptly leaves forest and enters an improbable little valley at a right angle to

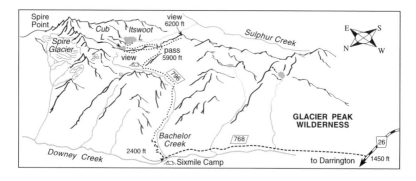

Cub Lake and Dome Peak from Bachelor Meadows

the main valley and just under Spire Point. Find water and flat campsites here in a scenic meadow.

For broader views, continue up the trail ½ mile through heather, following the small valley south to a 5900-foot pass. The trail drops ½
mile to 5338-foot Cub Lake and on down to 5015-foot Itswoot Lake.

Rather than descend, walk ¼ mile westward from the pass along a
narrow ridge to a superb view of Dome Peak and the glistening Dome
Glacier. A stone's throw below are the two lakes. South is Glacier
Peak. By camping on the ridge or at Cub Lake, one can explore
meadow slopes eastward to a 6200-foot ridge with an even more complete view of Dome.

11 MILK CREEK–DOLLY CREEK–VISTA CREEK LOOP

Loop trip 33 miles
Allow 3–5 days
High point 6000 feet
Elevation gain 4400 feet
Hikable mid-July through mid-October

Map: Green Trails No. 112
Glacier Peak
Current information: Ask at Darrington Ranger Station about trail Nos. 784, 790, and 2000

A section of the Pacific Crest Trail climbing high on the north flanks of Glacier Peak. Massive flower fields and close-up views of the mountain. Plan to spend an extra day, at least, roaming alpine ridges.

Drive Suiattle River road No. 26 (Hike 7) 23 miles to the end, elevation 1600 feet. Walk the abandoned road 1 mile to a Y; take the right fork. The Milk Creek trail drops a few steps and crosses the river on a bridge. The way begins in glorious forest; at a mile or so is an awesome grove of ancient and huge cedars, hemlocks, and Douglas firs. Going sometimes level, sometimes uphill, passing cold streams, the path rounds a ridge into the valley of Milk Creek.

The trail enters a broad field of greenery at 3 miles, 2400 feet, with a stunning look up to the ice, a satisfying reward for a short trip. A pleasant campsite in the forest by the river is ½ mile before the field.

From here the trail ascends gently, then passes campsites in the woods, and meets the Pacific Crest Trail at 7½ miles, 3900 feet. Turn left at the junction and plod upward on a series of 36 switchbacks (growing views of Glacier Peak and toward Mica Lake and Fire Mountain) to the crest of Milk Creek Ridge at 11½ miles, 6000 feet. Here a climbers' route to the summit of Glacier leaves the trail, which traverses the flowery basin of the East Fork Milk Creek headwaters, crosses a ridge into the source of Dolly Creek, and at 14 miles comes to Vista Ridge and a camp, 5500 feet.

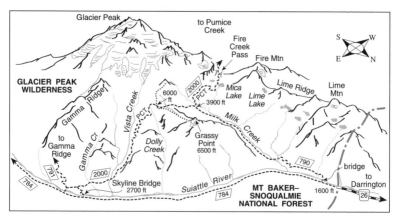

Flower gardens spread in every direction and views are grand north to Miners Ridge, Plummer Mountain, Dome Peak, and beyond. Glacier Peak is too close to be seen at its best. The trip schedule should include one or more walking-around days from the Vista Ridge camp. Wander up the crest to a 7000-foot knoll. Even better, hike north in meadows to 6500-foot Grassy Point, offering views up and down the green valley of the Suiattle River, but especially of the white-glaciered volcano.

From the ridge the trail descends a long series of switchbacks into forest. At 20 miles, 3000 feet, is a campsite by the crossing of Vista Creek. At 21¼ miles is a junction with the Suiattle River trail and at 22 miles, 2700 feet, the trail crosses Skyline Bridge to Skyline Camp and proceeds 11 miles down the valley, reaching the road-end and completing the loop at 33 miles.

Glacier Peak and Milk Creek valley

12 IMAGE LAKE

Round trip 32 miles
Allow 2–3 days
High point 6100 feet
Elevation gain 4500 feet
Hikable mid-July through
October

Maps: Green Trails No. 112
GlacierPeak and No. 113 Holden
Current information: Ask at Dar-
rington Ranger Station about
trail Nos. 784 and 785

A 2-mile high volcano, the image of its glaciers reflected in an alpine tarn. Meadow ridges for dreamwalking. The long sweep of Suiattle River forests. Casting ballots with their feet, hikers have voted this a supreme climax of the alpine world of the North Cascades and the nation.

Drive Suiattle River road No. 26 (Hike 7) 23 miles to the end, elevation 1600 feet. Walk abandoned roadway 1 mile to a Y; go left on the Suiattle River trail, largely level, partly in ancient trees, partly in young trees, sometimes with looks to the river, crossing small tributaries, to Canyon Creek Camp, 6½ miles, 2300 feet. At about 9½ miles, 2800 feet, is a creek with a small campsite but no water by mid-summer. Just beyond is a trail junction; go left on Miners Ridge trail No. 785. The forest switchbacks are relentless and dry but with occasional glimpses, then spectacular views, out to the valley and the volcano. At 12½ miles are two welcome streams at the edge of meadow country and at 13 miles, 4800 feet, is a junction; campsites here.

Miners Cabin trail No. 795, leading to Suiattle Pass, goes straight ahead from the junction; take the left fork to Image Lake. Switchback up and up, into blueberry and flower meadows to expanding views, to a junction atop Miners Ridge, about 15 miles, 6150 feet. A ¼-mile trail leads to Miners Ridge Lookout, 6210 feet, the wilderness ranger's headquarters. The main trail goes right ¾ mile, traversing, then dropping a bit, to 6050-foot Image Lake.

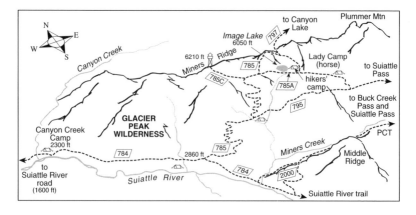

Sunset on Glacier Peak reflected in Image Lake

Solitude is not the name of the game here. Indeed, so dense is the summer population that the Forest Service, to protect fragile meadows, has prohibited camping around and above the lake to keep the water pure; it has banned swimming when the water is low. Below the lake ¼ mile is a hikers' camp (no campfires). A mile away at Lady Camp are accommodations for horses and mice. (On a bench above the trail look for the lovely lady carved in a tree by a sheepherder in about 1916.)

Exploring the basin, climbing the 6758-foot knoll above, visiting the fire lookout, walking the Canyon Lake trail into the headwaters of Canyon Creek—thus one may fill memorable days. By no means omit the finest wandering of all, along the wide crest of Miners Ridge, through flower gardens, looking north to Dome Peak and south across Suiattle forests to Glacier Peak.

Letters can and did make a difference. Kennecott Copper Corporation had planned to dig a ½-mile-wide open-pit mine 1 mile east of the lake at Lady Camp Basin. This blasphemy was prevented by violent objections from citizen-hikers who wrote letters to congress members and senators.

From Lady Camp the trail drops some 500 feet in ½ mile to a junction with the Suiattle Pass trail, which can be followed 1¾ miles back to the Image Lake trail junction.

13

SUIATTLE RIVER
TO LAKE CHELAN

One-way trip 29½ miles
Allow 5–7 days
High point 6438 feet
Elevation gain about 5000 feet
Hikable mid-July through
September

Maps: Green Trails No. 112
Glacier Peak, No. 113 Holden,
and No. 114 Lucerne
Current information: Ask at Darrington Ranger Station about
trail Nos. 784, 786, and 2000 and
Chelan Ranger Station about
trail Nos. 1256 and 1240

A rich, extended sampler of the Glacier Peak Wilderness, beginning
in green-mossy westside trees, rising to flowers of Miners Ridge and
views of Glacier Peak, crossing Suiattle and Cloudy Passes, descending
parklands of Lyman Lake to rainshadow forests of Railroad Creek and
Lake Chelan. The traverse can be done in either direction; the west-to-
east route is described here.

Drive to the Suiattle River road-end, 1600 feet, and hike 11 miles on
the Suiattle River trail to the 4800-foot junction with the Image Lake
trail (Hike 12).

Continue straight ahead on Miners Cabin trail No. 795, climbing 1¾
miles to a second junction with the Image Lake trail, 5500 feet. (The
lake can—and should, if time allows—be included in the trip by taking
the lake trail, which is 4½ miles from end to end, thus adding some 3
extra miles and about 600 feet of extra elevation gained and lost.) In
trees just past the junction are abandoned miners' shacks that are
starting to collapse and a spring, a bad-weather campsite. The way
now contours, crossing one huge and many small avalanche paths, entering open slopes with grand views to Fortress, Chiwawa, and other
peaks at the head of Miners Creek, passing more miners' junk in a

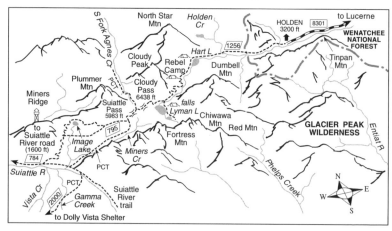

small flat. The way briefly joins the Pacific Crest Trail and, at 17 miles, reaches Suiattle Pass, 5983 feet. A bit before the pass and below the trail is a pleasant camp on a meadow bench.

The trail drops some 300 feet into headwaters of South Fork Agnes Creek (when the snow is gone the drop can be partially avoided by taking a rough hiker-only alternate path) and climbs to the most spectacular views and gardens of the trip at 6438-foot Cloudy Pass, 19 miles. (From here, easy meadows demand a sidetrip to 7915-foot Cloudy Peak and along the ridge toward 8068-foot North Star Mountain.)

Descend through magnificent flowers, then subalpine forest, to 5587-foot Lyman Lake, 21 miles. Campsites are in the woods north of the lake and at the outlet, but camps above, under Cloudy Peak, have better views and fewer bugs. If you build a campfire, use an existing fire ring. From the lake outlet, a hiker-only trail climbs 500 feet to

Lyman Lake

Upper Lyman Lake (Hike 98). At the lake begin bear problems that continue the full length of the Railroad Creek valley; look to the defense of your good things.

The trail drops past the outlet creek of Lyman Lake, where frothy water pours down long, clean granite slabs, and switchbacks into forests of Railroad Creek; views of Crown Point Falls and Hart Lake. After boggy walking and several bridges, at 24½ miles, 3989 feet, is Rebel Camp and at 25½ miles is Hart Lake. Both have good camping.

The last portion of the route is over blocks of rock under a tall cliff, past tumbling waterfalls, occasional views of high peaks, to beaver bottom and green jungle, and finally a jeep track and baseball field to the abandoned mining town of Holden, 19½ miles, 3200 feet.

Holden Village, Inc., uses the old town as a religious retreat but may sell a hiker ice cream. A road goes 12 miles down to Lucerne, on Lake Chelan, a hot and dusty walk; alternatively, hike trail No. 1240 past Domke Lake to Lucerne (Hike 96). From May 15 to October 15 (check with the Forest Service–Park Service Information Center in Seattle) a bus from Lucerne Resort makes four daily round trips, permitting hikers to catch the *Lady of the Lake* downlake to Chelan (Hike 96) and a bus home.

14 AROUND GLACIER PEAK

One-way trip (north and east sections) 52 miles
Allow 5 days minimum
High point 6409 feet (Little Giant Pass)
Elevation gain 9800 feet

One-way trip (south and west sections) 44 miles
Allow 5 days minimum
High point 6450 feet (Red Pass)
Elevation gain 5700 feet

Hikable late July through September
Maps: Green Trails No. 111 Sloan Peak, No. 112 Glacier Peak, and No. 113 Holden
Current information: Ask at Darrington Ranger Station about trail Nos. 784, 2000, 789, and 790 and Lake Wenatchee Ranger Station about trail Nos. 1513, 1518, 1562, and 1507

Mount Rainier National Park has the Wonderland Trail; the Glacier Peak Wilderness offers an equally classic and less crowded around-the-mountain hike. The 96-mile circuit with an estimated 15,500 feet of climbing includes virgin forests, glacial streams, alpine meadows, and ever-changing views of the "last wild volcano."

The complete trip requires a minimum of 10 days, and this makes no allowance for explorations and bad-weather layovers. However, the

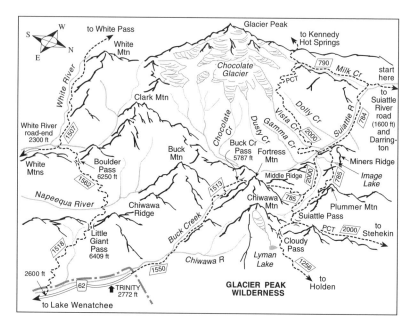

Indian Head Peak from White Pass

loop breaks logically into two sections which can be taken separately. Perhaps the ideal schedule is to do the entire circuit on a single 2-week jaunt, keeping packs to a reasonable weight by arranging to be met midway with additional supplies.

North and East Sections

Begin at the Suiattle River road-end (Hike 13). Hike 11 miles along the Suiattle River on trail No. 784 to a junction with Pacific Crest Trail No. 2000. Go left on the PCT 4½ miles, then right on Middle Ridge trail No. 789 another 5 miles to Buck Creek Pass.

(Two partial alternate routes can be taken; each adds a day and many extra rewards. One is the Milk Creek–Dolly Creek–Vista Creek loop (Hike 11), which adds 12 miles and 3200 feet of elevation gain to the total. The other is the Image Lake–Miners Ridge trail (Hike 12), which adds 8 miles and 1700 feet of elevation gain.)

Puffball mushrooms

Descend 9½ miles from Buck Creek Pass to Trinity (Hike 71) and walk the Chiwawa River road to Little Giant trail No. 1518. (Note: River crossing problems are described in Hikes 70 and 65. Due to the road walking and missing bridges, hikers may prefer to drive between Trinity and the White River trailhead.) Climb 4½ miles over Little Giant Pass and descend 1¾ miles to a ford of the Napeequa River. Cross the river and follow Boulder Pass trail No. 1562 some 22 miles over the pass and down to White River trail No. 1507. (If this trail is impassable, use Indian Creek trail No. 1502, Hike 64.) If the trip is to be broken at this point, hike 3½ miles downriver to the White River road.

The itinerary (excluding the alternates) would be as follows: Day One, 11 miles and a 1150-foot climb to Miners Creek (the best camping is on the river ¼ mile beyond Miners Creek); Day Two, 9½ miles and a 3200-foot climb to Buck Creek Pass; Day Three, descend 3350 feet in 15 miles to Maple Creek; Day Four, climb 3900 feet, descend 2300 feet, in the 6½ miles to the Napeequa River; Day Five, 10 miles to the White River road-end, a climb of 1550 feet and a descent of 3350 feet. However, frequent campsites along the route allow shorter days or different days.

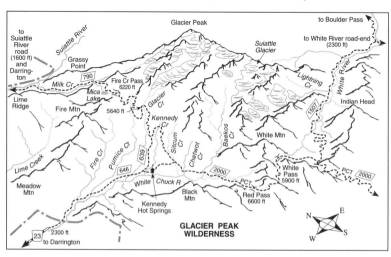

South and West Sections

Begin at the White River road-end. Hike 14¼ miles on White River trail No. 1507 to an intersection with the Pacific Crest Trail. Continue north on the crest 2 miles to White Pass (Hike 64).

From White Pass contour and climb to Red Pass in 2 miles, then descend the White Chuck River (Hike 20) 7 miles to a junction. For the main route, climb right on the Pacific Crest Trail, crossing headwaters of Kennedy Creek, Glacier Creek, Pumice Creek, and Fire Creek and reaching Fire Creek Pass in 8 miles (Hike 18).

(For an inviting alternate, go 2 miles from the junction downriver to Kennedy Hot Springs, enjoy a warm (90-degree) bath, then continue a short ½ mile to the Kennedy Ridge trail (Hike 17) and climb to rejoin the main route; this alternate adds 2½ miles and 800 feet of elevation gain to the total.)

From Fire Creek Pass, the snowiest part of the entire circuit, descend a valley of moraines and ponds, past the magnificent cold cirque of Mica Lake, reaching the Dolly–Vista trail junction in 4 miles. Continue 7½ miles down Milk Creek trail to the Suiattle River road-end (Hike 11).

A possible itinerary would be as follows: Day One, 9 miles and 800 feet elevation gain to Lightning Creek; Day Two, 9¼ miles, a gain of 2100 feet and a loss of 1000 feet, to Glacier Peak Meadows; Day Three, drop 1700 feet and climb 2250 feet on the 9½ miles to Pumice Creek; Day Four, 500 feet up and 900 feet down in 4½ miles to Mica Lake; Day Five, 11 miles and 3800 feet down to Suiattle River road. Again, frequent campsites allow shorter or different days.

Ptarmigan

Peek-A-Boo Lake

SAUK RIVER
Unprotected area

PEEK-A-BOO LAKE

Round trip 6 miles
Hiking time 4 hours
High point 4300 feet
Elevation gain 1300 feet in,
400 feet out
Hikable July through October

One day or backpack
Map: Green Trails No. 111 Sloan
Peak
Current information: Ask at Dar-
rington Ranger Station about
trail No. 656

A forest trail climbs to a delightful meadow with a spectacular view, then drops to a lake set in the deep woods of a deep cirque.

From Darrington, drive the Mountain Loop Highway, road No. 20, along the west side of the Sauk River. At 8.8 miles (just short of the

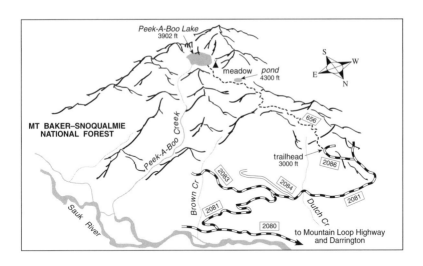

Sauk River bridge), turn right on road No. 2080 for 1.1 miles and turn right again on road No. 2081, signed "Peek-A-Boo Lake 4 miles." At 4.5 miles from the highway go left on road No. 2086 and at 5.7 miles from the highway find the trailhead at a wide parking area and turnaround, elevation 3000 feet.

Peek-A-Boo Lake trail No. 656 climbs along an old logging grade ⅓ mile, then narrows to a footpath in virgin forest. Note the stumps with springboard notches from logging operations of the late 1940s.

Relentless switchbacks ascend to a 4300-foot high point from which easy ups and downs lead to a small pond and a pretty meadow. For the trip climax, leave the trail and cross the meadow to the spectacular viewpoint of White Chuck Mountain and Mt. Pugh. Look down better than half a vertical mile to the Sauk River and out to the White Chuck River. The glacier-white summit of Dome Peak stands over Meadow Ridge, and Mt. Shuksan rises in the distance.

From the meadow the trail deteriorates to a boot-beaten path as it descends 400 feet to the lakeshore and campsites, 3902 feet.

Mount Pugh from Peek-A-Boo Lake trail

16   CRYSTAL LAKE

Round trip 8 miles
Allow 6 hours
High point 4485 feet
Elevation gain 2200 feet in,
300 feet out
Wilderness regulations at lake
Hikable late June through
October

Map: Green Trails No. 111 Sloan
Peak
Current information: Ask at Dar-
rington Ranger Station about
trail Nos. 657 and 638

A pleasant mountain lake in meadows surrounded by forested ridges, reached by miles of walking a long-abandoned logging road covered by thick brush and alders, a stiff climb on a fire line, and finally ½ mile of true trail to the lake, which is a meager ¼ mile within Glacier Peak Wilderness. It is permissible to employ vile language discussing the 1960s foresters who clearcut-obliterated this and many other trails and never restored them.

Drive the Mountain Loop Highway from Darrington. At roughly 9 miles cross the Sauk River on a concrete bridge. Pass road No. 22 and in 0.2 mile beyond the bridge go left on White Chuck road No. 23 for 6 miles, then left on road No. 2700 signed "Meadow Mountain Trail 3 miles." At 2.4 miles (not 3 as the road sign says) find the unsigned trailhead on your right, elevation 2580 feet.

The road, formerly No. 2710, now trail No. 657, climbs 450 feet, with glimpses of White Chuck, Pugh, and Glacier lightening the load, then loses 300 feet. At 1⅓ miles go left on the obscure, overgrown Crystal Creek road. The only sign, almost hidden in brush, is "Road No. (2710)011." (The main road goes to Meadow Mountain (Hike 17)).

The steadily climbing road, now trail No. 638, is brushing in fast and

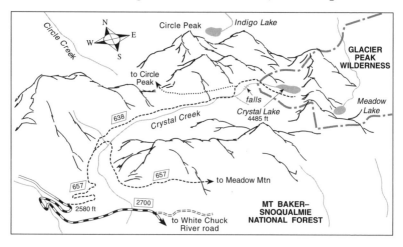

Crystal Lake

may soon be lost (hikers, do a good deed and carry your loppers). At about 1½ miles from Meadow Mountain trail (road), 3600 feet, the good grade ends in a pleasant campsite beside Crystal Creek. In the next ½ mile the road-trail deteriorates to a muddy rut through the brush, ending at the far end of a clearcut 3½ miles from the car. From here the route goes straight up 500 feet on what was once a fire line. The agony is eased by sound and sight of nearby waterfalls.

At the top of the clearcut the fire line intersects the old Crystal Lake–Circle Peak trail (Hike 7). The ascent continues but the unmolested forest and true trail make the remaining scant ½ mile to Crystal Lake a breeze. Wilderness regulations apply at the lake.

17

MEADOW MOUNTAIN– FIRE MOUNTAIN

**Round trip to 5800-foot viewpoint
16 miles
Allow 2 days
High point 5800 feet
Elevation gain 3500 feet in,
300 feet out**

**One-way trip to White Chuck
River road-end 21 miles
Allow 2–4 days
High point 6000 feet
Elevation gain 4000 feet**

**Hikable July through October
Maps: Green Trails No. 111 Sloan Peak and No. 112 Glacier Peak
Current information: Ask at Darrington Ranger Station about trail
No. 657**

Meadows laced with alpine trees, views to White Chuck forests and Glacier Peak ice, and a long parkland ridge for roaming, plus sidetrips to cirque lakes. But be warned: there is a 4½-mile walk to the trailhead on an abandoned road covered by dense brush and alders. Some of the misery is compensated for by spectacular views of Mt. Pugh and Glacier Peak.

From Darrington drive the Mountain Loop Highway 9 miles, turn left on White Chuck River road No. 23 for 5.5 miles, then left on road

Glacier Peak from side of Meadow Mountain

No. 2700 another 2.4 miles, and park at the beginning of the Meadow Mountain road-trail, elevation 2580 feet (Hike 16).

Walk road No. 2710 (now trail No. 657), passing the Crystal Creek road-trail at 1⅓ miles, and cross Crystal Creek to reach the genuine trail at 4½ miles, elevation 3400 feet.

The trail climbs a steep 1¼ miles (but in deep, cool forest) to the first meadow. Cross a bubbling brook in an open basin and choose either of two destinations, both offering splendid views down to the green valley and out to the peaks. For the easiest, follow a faint way trail 1 mile westward toward a high knoll. For the best and the most flowers, hike the main trail 2 miles eastward, climbing to a 5800-foot spur ridge from Meadow Mountain.

For one of the great backpacking ridge walks in the Glacier Peak Wilderness, take the up-and-down trail traversing the ridge east toward Fire Mountain. Earlier camps are possible, but the first site with guaranteed all-summer water is Owl Creek at 8½ miles, in a bouldery basin to which the trail drops to avoid cliffs of Meadow Mountain.

Going up, then down, then up again, at 10¼ miles the trail touches the 5850-foot ridge crest. For a sidetrip, descend 1 mile northwest on a much-used but indistinct and easily lost path to 5300-foot Diamond Lake. From the east shore climb a wide gully up the low ridge and descend extremely steep slopes (no trail) to Emerald Lake, 5200 feet. Good camps at Diamond Lake; stay 100 feet from the shores.

The main trail continues along the ridge to a low saddle and proceeds east through patches of trees, grassy swales, sidehill flowers, and views. At 12 miles, beneath Fire Mountain, are charming garden camps near the site of long-gone Fire Chief Shelter. From this area experienced off-trail travelers can find an easy but not obvious route to the summit of 6591-foot Fire Mountain; if the terrain gets steep and scary, you've gone wrong—turn back.

The trail descends an old burn to Fire Creek forests, joining the White Chuck River trail at 16½ miles, 1½ miles from the White Chuck River road. By use of two cars, one parked at each road-end, hikers can enjoy a 21-mile one-way trip along the full length of the ridge; a 3-day schedule allows for sidetrips, but more days could easily be spent exploring.

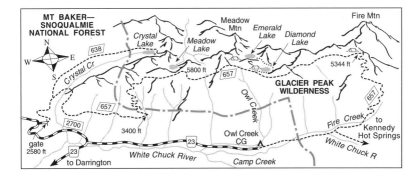

18 KENNEDY RIDGE AND HOT SPRINGS

Round trip to Kennedy Hot Springs 11 miles
Hiking time 5 hours
High point 3300 feet
Elevation gain 1000 feet
Hikable May through November

Round trip to Kennedy Ridge (Glacier Creek campsite) 18 miles
Hiking time 8–10 hours
High point 5250 feet
Elevation gain 3000 feet
Hikable July through October

One day or backpack
Maps: Green Trails No. 111 Sloan Peak and No. 112 Glacier Peak
Current information: Ask at Darrington Ranger Station about trail Nos. 643 and 2000

Two hikes which can be done separately or combined. A short-and-low trip leads through tall, old trees, beside a roaring river, to volcano-warmed waters—the most mob-jammed spot in the Glacier Peak Wilderness. A long-and-high trip climbs to alpine flowers and a close look at icefalls tumbling from Glacier Peak.

Drive White Chuck River road No. 23 (Hike 16) 10 miles to the road-end parking area and campground, elevation 2300 feet.

The wide, gentle White Chuck River trail has become—deservedly—the most popular valley walk in the Glacier Peak area. The way goes through virgin forest always near and sometimes beside the ice-fed river, beneath striking cliffs of volcanic tuff, crossing the frothing tributaries of Fire, Pumice, and Glacier Creeks. At 5 miles, 3300 feet, is a junction with the hot springs and Kennedy Ridge trails.

Kennedy Hot Springs: In 1976 and in 1990 floods ravaged the White Chuck River trail to Kennedy Creek. The trail has been restored to the guard station, hot springs, and camp, 3300 feet. The beautiful forest is the proper reward of hiking to Kennedy, but an amazing percentage of the 6000 people who annually sign the register come for the hot (actually only warm) springs. To satisfy geological curiosity, cross the river on a bridge, turn left, and in a few yards come to the cruddy, rusty waters seeping from the earth. A tublike pool has been dug, just big enough for three or four people who don't believe in the germ theory of disease. The waiting line gets long at the pool in good weather. It would be a lot shorter if folks knew that in summer the coliform bacteria count exceeds that of the average sewer.

Kennedy Ridge: From the junction at 5 miles, just before crossing Kennedy Creek, climb left on the Kennedy Ridge trail. (A full canteen is barely adequate.) The steep forest way, occasionally glimpsing ice above, joins the Pacific Crest Trail at 2 miles, 4150 feet. The Crest Trail switchbacks through cliffs of red and gray andesite, then along heather parklands on a moraine crest, swinging left to reach the welcome splash (and campsite) of Glacier Creek at 5650 feet, 4 miles from the White Chuck River trail.

Glacier Peak from Kennedy Ridge

Leave the trail and climb open subalpine forests on the old moraine, then in ½ mile step suddenly out onto raw boulders of a much newer moraine. See the Kennedy and Scimitar Glaciers tumbling down the volcano.

It's a shame to turn back at the edge of so much good highland roaming. Just 1 mile from Glacier Creek, over Glacier Ridge, are the splendid meadows and camps of Pumice Creek, and in 3½ miles more is Fire Creek Pass.

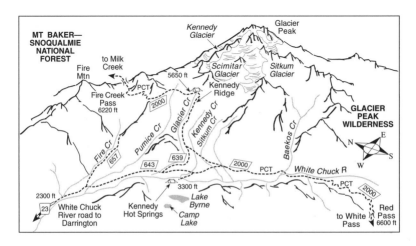

19

LAKE BYRNE

Round trip 16 miles
Allow 2–3 days
High point 5544 feet
Elevation gain 3200 feet
Hikable August through
September

Maps: Green Trails No. 111 Sloan
Peak and No. 112 Glacier Peak
Current information: Ask at Dar-
rington Ranger Station about
trail Nos. 643 and 774

In olden times, when it took 2 full days of hiking up the White Chuck River just to get to Kennedy Hot Springs, pedestrians never devoted less than a week to the trip. The glorious forest was savored fully. The springs were much enjoyed after sessions of trail-sweating, and with relative safety, the bathers being few and their diseases not

Lake Byrne and Glacier Peak

terribly fearsome. However, the cherry on the tip of the whipped cream was Lake Byrne and the highland roaming westward from there. For modern weekenders, however, backpacking to the lake is something of a horror story. The last chapter, the trail from hot springs to lake, is short, but *steep*. And spots near the lake where a sleeping bag can be spread are so few that some campers pitch tents on the lake itself, which is usually frozen solid all but a few weeks of late summer. No fires permitted, of course. The recommendation, therefore, is to basecamp at Kennedy and day-hike to the lake and the meadow ridges above.

Drive White Chuck River road No. 23 (Hike 16) 10 miles to the road-end parking area and campground, elevation 2300 feet.

Hike 5½ miles to the patrol cabin at Kennedy Hot Springs (Hike 18) and find a campsite on either side of the White Chuck River, 3300 feet.

From the patrol cabin cross the footbridge to a junction. The left fork goes 100 yards to the warm (80–90 degree) springs, which you will not wish to put your own body in but which may contain bodies worth looking at. The right fork climbs a bit, past campsites, and then takes dead aim on the sky, gaining 2200 feet in the next 2½ miles. The good news is that horses try it so rarely that the tread is well preserved.

The first 1¼ miles from the hot springs are well shaded, with glimpses through chinks in the green wall of the blinding snows of Glacier Peak. A fairly level and quite brief respite from steepness has heather meadows, a small stream, and possible camping. Then, upward again, the views get bigger and the trail poorer. At 2½ miles from the hot springs, 8 miles from the road, is Lake Byrne, 5544 feet.

The shores are mostly steep heather meadows, rockslides, cliffs, and snowfields. The few campsites are widely scattered around parkland knolls; if you arrive late on a busy weekend, inspect your chosen spot to see whether campers on the other side of the knoll have been using it for other purposes.

For meadows that grow wider and views that expand constantly, take the right fork at the lakeshore and climb 500 feet more to a viewpoint overlooking Camp Lake, set in a deep, cold little bowl where the sun rarely shines and the snow hardly ever melts.

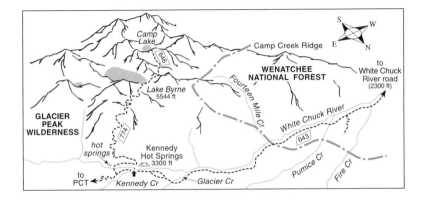

Glacier Peak from White Mountain

WHITE CHUCK RIVER
Glacier Peak Wilderness

20   WHITE CHUCK GLACIER

**Round trip to Glacier Peak
  Meadows 24 miles
Allow 4 days minimum
High point about 5400 feet
Elevation gain 3100 feet
Hikable late July through
  September**

**Maps: Green Trails No. 111 Sloan
  Peak and No. 112 Glacier Peak
Current information: Ask at Darrington Ranger Station about
  trail Nos. 643 and 2000**

Begin beside a loud river in deep forest. Walk miles through big trees; climb to little trees and wide meadows. Roam flowers and water-falls and moraines to a broad glacier. Wander gardens and ridges. In the opinion of some experts, this is the supreme low-to-high tour of the Glacier Peak Wilderness.

Drive to the White Chuck River road-end, 2300 feet, and hike 5½ miles to 3300-foot Kennedy Hot Springs (Hike 18).

Ascend steeply then gently to join the Pacific Crest Trail at Sitkum Creek, 3850 feet, 7 miles from the road; camping space is available here when Kennedy is full-up, as it often is. The Crest Trail continues along the valley, passing the avalanche track and meadow-marsh of Chetwot Creek, fording Baekos Creek, and at 9½ miles, 4200 feet, crossing a high bridge over the rocky chasm and thundering falls of the White Chuck River.

Now the trail climbs a valley step. Trees are smaller and so is the river, assembling itself from snow-fed tributaries. A little meadow gives promise of what lies above. After more subalpine forest, the way enters the tremendous open basin of Glacier Peak Meadows. At 12 miles, 5400 feet, is the site of the long-gone Glacier Peak Shelter, magnificent campsites everywhere around.

As a base for easy hiker-type explorations, this highland valley of flowers and creeks and snowfields is unsurpassed in the North Cascades.

First off, if your hike is mid-August or later, visit the ice; before that it is covered with snow. Climb meadows around the valley corner east, taking any of many appealing routes to a chilly flatland of moss and meanders, to moraines and meltwater, and finally the White Chuck Glacier. The white plateau is tempting, but only climbers with rope and ice ax should venture on its surface.

For another trip, investigate the intriguing White Chuck Cinder Cone, the remnant of a volcano smaller and newer than Glacier Peak. Scramble meadows higher to the 6999-foot summit of Portal Peak.

If your visit is in late July or early August it is flower time on White Mountain. Therefore, hike the Crest Trail 2 miles up a wintry, rocky basin to 6450-foot Red Pass; from here, continue on the trail to White Pass (in early July be careful of the steep snow slopes) or leave the trail and scramble to the summit of 7030-foot White Mountain.

Every direction calls. Invent your own wanderings. The minimum trip to the glacier can be done in 3 days but any itinerary of less than a week will leave the visitor frustrated, determined to return soon to finish the job at leisure.

Campsites other than those mentioned above are plentiful along the trail and throughout the high basin. However, as a conservation rule to be followed here and everywhere, camp only in established sites, not in the actual meadows, which are so fragile that only a few nights of camping can destroy nature's work of decades.

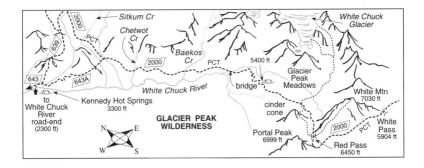

21 LOST CREEK RIDGE

Round trip to Round Lake view-point 10 miles	**Round trip to Lake Byrne 24 miles**
Hiking time 6–8 hours	**Allow 3 days minimum**
High point 5600 feet	**High point 6000 feet**
Elevation gain 3800 feet	**Elevation gain about 6500 feet**
Hikable July through October	**Hikable August through October**

One day or backpack
Map: Green Trails No. 111 Sloan Peak
**Current information: Ask at Darrington Ranger Station about trail
    No. 646**

A long ridge of green meadows, alpine lakes, and wide views of
peaks near and far—one of the most memorable highland trails in the
Glacier Peak region. The ridge can be ascended from either end for day
trips or overnight camps, or walked the full length on an extended
backpack. However, the middle section of the route is a boot-beaten
path, often overgrown. Particularly in the fog and snow, hikers must
be careful not to get lost on Lost Ridge (especially if there is much
snow on the ground).

Drive from Darrington on the Mountain Loop Highway 16 miles to
North Fork Sauk River road No. 49. Turn left 3 miles to a small parking area and trail sign, elevation 1849 feet.

The trail goes gently along the valley ½ mile, then climbs steeply
through open woods, with occasional views of impressive Sloan Peak,
to 4425-foot Bingley Gap, 3 miles. The way continues some 2 miles up
and along the ridge to meadows and a 5600-foot saddle overlooking

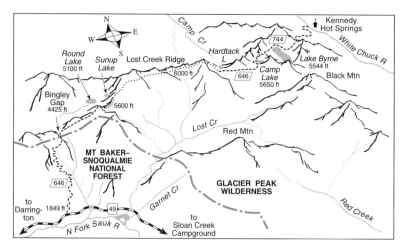

Sloan Peak and Lost Creek Ridge trail

Round Lake, 5100 feet. (A steep sidetrail descends to the lake and good camps.) Here is the place for day-trippers to have lunch, soak up the scenery, and return home; generally the trail is reasonably snowfree by early July.

Beyond this point is a stretch of route with only a faint tread. The practice used to be to build trail through patches of woods but leave travelers to find their own way across meadows. Routefinding is easiest when the snow is mostly gone, by late July. Though upsydownsy, the going is easy and glorious—always near or on the crest, mostly past vast meadows, through open basins, near small lakes, with constant and changing views, and a choice of delightful camps. Near Hardtack Lake continuous tread begins. At 11 miles, the trail now good, is 5650-foot Camp Lake, set in a cliff-walled cirque; near the lake is a gully that is extremely dangerous when full of snow. The trail climbs to a 6000-foot knob, drops a few feet to the rocky basin of "Little Siberia," then descends to famous Lake Byrne, 12 miles, 5544 feet. Flowers and rocks and waterfalls of the basin and adjoining ridges demand leisurely exploration, ever dominated by the tall white volcano rising beyond White Chuck River forests. However, campsites at Lake Byrne are so small, poor, and overused that exploration should be basecamped at Camp Lake or Kennedy Hot Springs. No campfires permitted at Lake Byrne.

From the lake the trail abruptly drops 2250 feet in 2 miles to Kennedy Hot Springs (Hike 18). If transportation can be arranged, such as by use of two cars, a 19-mile one-way trip can be done; allow 3 days or more.

SLOAN PEAK MEADOWS

Round trip 8 miles
Hiking time 7 hours
High point 4800 feet
Elevation gain 2900 feet
Hikable mid-July through
  September

One day or backpack
Map: Green Trails No. 111 Sloan
  Peak
Current information: Ask at Dar-
  rington Ranger Station about
  trail No. 648

The big-time, big-corporation prospectors of today racket about the sky in fleets of helicopters and never touch the ground except to drill holes in it and heap garbage on it. Their predecessors of 50 to 100 years ago, earthbound "dirty miners in search of shining gold," spent half their time building trails—often steep, but wide and solid enough for packtrains. Hundreds of miles of trails still in use were engineered

Cougar Creek

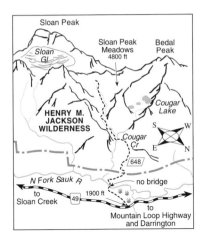

Rosy twisted stalk

by these old-timers, who never found gold or anything else of value, earned nothing for their sweat but a shirt that needed a bath.

One bit of their handiwork, the Cougar Creek trail, climbs from the North Fork Sauk River to meadows on the side of Sloan Peak. This would be a glorious spot to spend a couple of days roaming, but lacking dirty miners to maintain it, the trail has become so mean that hauling camping gear to the high country would try the cheerfulness of a Sherpa. Even as a day trip it's no simple stroll. Crossing the North Fork Sauk and Cougar Creek is always difficult and frequently impossible. If in doubt, return to the car and go someplace else, such as Lost Creek Ridge (Hike 21).

Drive from Darrington 16 miles on the Mountain Loop Highway to North Fork Sauk River road No. 49 and turn left 4.6 miles to the trailhead, signed "Sloane Peak Climbers' Trail," elevation 1900 feet.

Walk ½ mile to the river on abandoned road, in several places flooded by beaver ponds. The bridge is decades gone and unless a log-jam can be found upstream or down the trip is over—the river is much too deep and swift to ford safely.

On the far side of the river the trail follows an old logging railroad grade ¼ mile, then gains 500 feet up an old clearcut to the old miners' trail. Steep but wide, the relic ascends a long 2 miles to a rotten-log (obviously not permanent) crossing of Cougar Creek between two water-falls. In the next 2 miles the creek is crossed twice more—or perhaps not at all on a hot day when meltwater is roaring. The way continues relentlessly up, crossing four more creeks, each at the base of a waterfall. (Waterfalls are among the best parts of this hike.)

At a very long 4 miles, elevation 4800 feet, a small meadow invites camping, in views up to the Sloan Glacier and the summit cliffs of Sloan Peak and out east to Red Mountain and Glacier Peak. The slopes above the camp meadow invite wandering—which, however, should go only to the first steep snowfield unless the party has climbing gear and skills.

23 BALD EAGLE MOUNTAIN LOOP

Round trip 12 miles
Allow 1 day
High point 5200 feet
Elevation gain 2800 feet

Loop trip 24 miles plus 2½-mile
  walk on road
Allow 3 days
High point 6000 feet
Elevation gain 4000 feet

Hikable late July through September
Maps: Green Trails No. 111 Sloan Peak, No. 143 Monte Cristo, and No.
  144 Benchmark.
Current information: Ask at Darrington Ranger Station about trail
  Nos. 650 and 652

A spectacular day-hike view of Pride Basin and Monte Cristo peaks. Or a several-day looping ramble through miles of subalpine trees and meadows on lonesome trails traveled by more deer and marmots than people. The loop must be carefully planned to end each day at a campable ground—and water, which is scarce on the high ridges. After a spot at 1 mile on the abandoned road, the next for-sure water is at Spring Camp, 9 miles. However, early summer normally has snowbanks which cook up nicely in a pot.

Drive from Darrington 16 miles on the Mountain Loop Highway and turn left on North Fork Sauk River road No. 49. In 6.7 miles, pass road No. (4900)020 to the North Fork Sauk River trailhead, the end of the loop trip. Drive another 2.5 miles to a junction and horse ramp, and go right 0.5 mile more to the road-end at the footbridge across Sloan Creek, the beginning of Bald Eagle Mountain trail No. 650, elevation 2400 feet, the start of the loop trip. If the loop is planned, unload packs

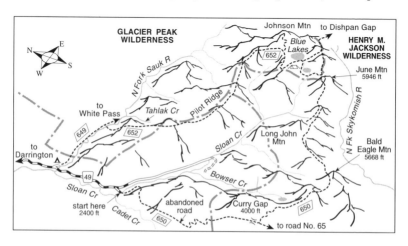

here and park the car back 2½ miles near the North Fork campground, where you'll be coming out.

Walk 2½ miles on a road converted to trail. Enter forest on a true trail and climb a sometimes muddy 1½ miles to Curry Gap, 4000 feet, and a junction with the Quartz Creek trail. Go left on Bald Eagle trail No. 650, climbing to the 5200-foot level of 5668-foot Bald Eagle Mountain and the turnaround for day-hikers. Dig out the lunch stuff and soak in the views of Pride Basin and the glaciers on the north sides of Kyes, Monte Cristo, and Cadet Peaks.

For the loop, pick up your pack and begin the ups and downs, past Long John Camp (often dry) at 8 miles from the road and Spring Camp at 9 miles. The trail then climbs within a few yards of the crest of 5946-foot June Mountain. Be sure to take the short sidetrip to the summit for views of Sloan Peak, Monte Cristo peaks, Glacier Peak, valleys, and forest. The tread on the north side of June Mountain may be covered by steep, hard snow. Take care.

At 12½ miles is a junction. The trail to the right continues 3 miles to Dishpan Gap and the Pacific Crest Trail. Go left on trail No. 652, dropping 500 feet, and at 14 miles reach 5500-foot Upper Blue Lake, usually frozen until mid-August; the best camps are near the upper lake.

From Upper Blue Lake the trail climbs 500 feet onto Pilot Ridge for 5 miles of some of the finest ridge-walking in the North Cascades. Finally the trail leaves the ridge and drops 3000 feet in an endless series of short, steep switchbacks to a ford and joins North Fork Sauk River trail No. 649, reaching Sloan Creek Campground at 11½ miles from Upper Blue Lake, 24 miles from the start.

Monte Cristo peaks from Pilot Ridge

2A STUJACK PASS (MOUNT PUGH)

Round trip to Stujack Pass 7½ miles
Hiking time 6–7 hours
High point 5500 feet
Elevation gain 3600 feet
Hikable mid-July through October

Round trip to Mt. Pugh 11 miles
Hiking time 10–12 hours
High point 7201 feet
Elevation gain 5300 feet
Hikable August through October

One day or backpack
Map: Green Trails No. 111 Sloan Peak
Current information: Ask at Darrington Ranger Station about trail No. 644

Positioned as it is so far west from the main mountain mass, Pugh's height and detachment make it strikingly tall and imposing—and an exceptional viewpoint. See out to lowlands of the Whulge (the original residents' name for "the saltwater"). See the North Cascades from Baker to Eldorado to Dome to Bonanza. See nearby Glacier Peak standing magnificently tall above White Chuck River forests. Closer, see the superb horn of Sloan and the sharp peaks of the Monte Cristo area. A rare panorama indeed, but not for everyone—the upper portion of the trail once led to a fire lookout but has long been abandoned and now is climbers' terrain. However, hikers can go most of the way and see most of the horizons.

Drive from Darrington on the Mountain Loop Highway 12.6 miles to Mt. Pugh road No. 2095 (may be signed "095"). Turn left 1 mile to the Mt. Pugh trail sign, elevation 1900 feet.

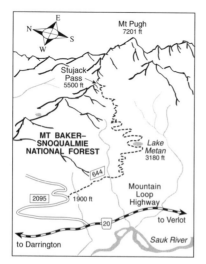

The steep trail climbs cool forest 1½ miles to tiny Lake Metan, 3180 feet, and the first outward looks. Relentless switchbacks ascend to meadows, 3 miles, beyond which point the trail is not maintained. The only decent camps on the route are here, but water may be gone by late summer.

Three Fingers and Whitehorse appear beyond valley forests as the trail switchbacks up talus and flowers to the notch of Stujack Pass, 3¾ miles, 5500 feet. Inexperienced travelers should have lunch and turn back, content with a full bag of scenery.

Those who go beyond Stujack

Mount Pugh

(named for its discovers, Stuart and Jackson, Coast and Geodetic surveyors who mapped the area a century or so ago) must be trained and equipped for steep snow (early summer) and for rock scrambling (all summer) where sections of trail have slid out. The abandoned trail climbs abruptly from the pass to a knife-edge rock ridge, then picks a delicate way along cliffs above a glacier trough, perhaps vanishing occasionally in snowfields. Part of the trail was dynamited from rock to provide access to the summit lookout; the first cabin was destroyed by lightning, and its successor was burned several decades ago. Steep heather and rock slabs lead to the summit, 5½ miles, 7201 feet.

The summit views are worth the effort for travelers who can use ice ax, hands and feet, and perhaps rope and thus manage the upper "trail" in safety. The views short of the summit are also worthwhile; be sure to stop, satisfied, when the going gets spooky.

25 BEDAL BASIN

Round trip 6 miles
Hiking time 6 hours
High point 5000 feet
Elevation gain 2200 feet
Hikable July through October
One day or backpack

Map: Green Trails No. 111 Sloan
   Peak
Current information: Ask at Dar-
   rington Ranger Station about
   trail No. 705

Lovely and lonesome alpine meadows beneath the towering south wall of Sloan Peak. The long-abandoned miners' trail is rough and sketchy, recommended only for experienced hikers who don't mind sweating a bit for the sake of solitude. Don't panic if there are half a dozen cars at the trailhead, which is also the start of a climbing route for Sloan Peak. (Climbers are not dangerous if you do not feed them.)

Drive from Darrington 17.3 miles (0.8 mile beyond the North Fork Sauk River bridge) and turn left on road No. 4096 for 3 miles to its present end, elevation about 2800 feet. Locate trail No. 705 on the up-hill side of the road.

The trail gains altitude steadily, alternating between cool forest and sun-hot avalanche tracks choked with ferns, salmonberry bushes, and a spicing of nettles. Occasionally the Forest Service sends a brushing crew up the lower trail, which thus is better walking some years than others. If a crew hasn't been along recently, be prepared to foot-probe blindly for the tread in shoulder-high greenery.

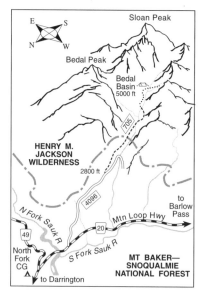

At 1½ miles, amid big trees beside the creek, is a campsite much-used by Sloan climbers of years past. Cross Bedal Creek here—hopefully on a log. The way gentles out in a broad avalanche area of alder and vine maple and a gathering of tributaries. At 2 miles recross the creek.

The trail becomes obscure (unless the Forest Service unexpectedly takes up the job started by Harry Bedal many decades ago). The route is steep, ascending an abrupt valley step. Faint tread gains a few hundred feet along the left side of the creek, now quite small, crosses to the right side, and—probably—vanishes. If so, continue upward several hundred feet, cross the creek to the left side, and climb open timber.

When the left side gets brushy, cross to forest on the right side and ascend huckleberry slopes to a collapsed mine with a stream flowing from the mouth. About 100 feet higher, rediscover the faint trail, which contours right, into open meadows at the lip of the basin, 5000 feet.

Above is the wall of Sloan. Monster boulders fringe the heather-and-flower floor of the basin. Near a great block of rock on the right side of the meadow are rotten logs of Harry Bedal's cabin, which along about 1940 succumbed to the crushing winter snows. Splendid camps all around. From the pass at the basin head are broad views.

Harry Bedal's cabin

26   GOAT LAKE

Round trip 10 miles
Hiking time 5 hours
High point 3161 feet
Elevation gain 1280 feet
Hikable mid-June through
  October

One day or backpack
Map: Green Trails No. 111 Sloan
  Peak
Current information: Ask at Dar-
  rington Ranger Station about
  trail No. 647

A subalpine lake beneath cliffs and glaciers, a popular destination with hikers of all ages. Wander beside clear, cold water, investigate artifacts of long-ago mining, and admire snow-fed waterfalls frothing down rock walls. The trail (foot travel only) partly traces the route of a wagon road dating from the late nineteenth century.

Drive from Verlot on the Mountain Loop Highway, at 20 miles crossing Barlow Pass and descending into the South Fork Sauk River valley. At 3.5 miles from the pass, turn right on Elliott Creek road No. 4080 and drive 0.8 mile to the trailhead parking lot, elevation 1900 feet.

Once the trail was within sight of Elliott Creek, but heavy hiker use has turned swampy areas into huge impassable quagmires. Until repairs are made, trail No. 647 follows an abandoned logging road shaded by young alder trees. At 3½ miles the road ends and the way drops a bit to follow the all-but-vanished route of a wagon road that once reached the mining settlement and hotel near Goat Lake.

At approximately 4 miles from the parking area the trail enters the Henry M. Jackson Wilderness. At 4½ miles the trail leaves the wagon road, steepens, and switchbacks upward, reaching the outlet of Goat Lake at 5 miles, elevation 3161 feet.

For an interesting sidetrip, at 4½ miles, where the old wagon route diverges rightward from the trail, cross Elliott Creek to decrepit

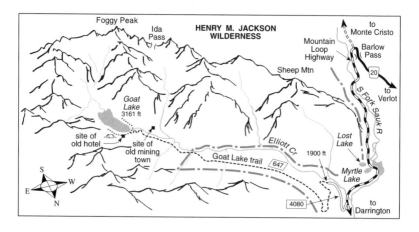

Goat Lake

remains of a mining settlement. The wagon route then switchbacks and in roughly ½ mile recrosses the creek on risky remnants of a bridge to meet the trail.

Enjoy the views of Foggy Peak. Prowl relics of what was, some 75 years ago, a busy mining town. In summer sunshine, take a brisk swim.

Beyond the outlet is a nice spot to picnic. The trail continues left around the shore, eventually disappearing in alder and vine maple. On a rocky knoll before the brush is a particularly fine place to sit and stare and eat lunch before going home.

Because campers have overused the lakeshore areas, these are now restricted to picnicking. At the old hotel site are four to six campsites on a knoll above the outlet. Along Elliott Creek is a spacious group campsite; enquire at the ranger station. Fires are prohibited.

27 GOTHIC BASIN

Round trip from Barlow Pass
   10 miles
Hiking time 11 hours
High point 5000 feet
Elevation gain 2600 feet
Hikable late July through early
   October

One day or backpack
Maps: Green Trails No. 111 Sloan
   Peak and No. 143 Monte Cristo
Current information: Ask at Dar-
   rington Ranger Station about
   trail No. 724

Glacier-rounded buttresses of brown limestone, ice-plucked walls of bleached granite, scratched and polished sandstone and conglomerate, and rusty streaks that tantalized a prospector generation. Plus water-falls in slot gorges, snow-cold ponds in rock scoops, an Arctic-barren cirque lake, and amid all the shivering, meadow bits that in summer are heather-blossom-red and in fall huckleberry-blue.

From 1909 to 1912 the Northwest Mining Company poured a fortune into operating a 7000-foot aerial tram from Weden House, on the Monte Cristo Railroad line, to a mine below the basin lip. The rust contained no mineral more valuable than iron oxide, the railroad also was a loser, and the headwaters of the South Fork Sauk reverted to wildness. Then, in the 1940s, the Manifest Destiny of the automobile generated a road. Then, in 1980, the Sauk River expressed *its* Manifest Destiny.

Drive 19.5 miles from the Verlot Public Service Center to Barlow Pass, 2360 feet.

Walk past the gate on the Monte Cristo road-that-was a scant 1 mile to rickety bridges over the river and just before the crossing find the trailhead, elevation 2400 feet.

The first mile is the contribution to pedestrian America by Will Thompson and Volunteers for Outdoor Washington (VOW), who roughed out a rude route to avoid the old trail's start from Weden House, which involved somehow crossing the river. Once intersected, the old trail is worse than rude, it's hardly there at all, eroded to a

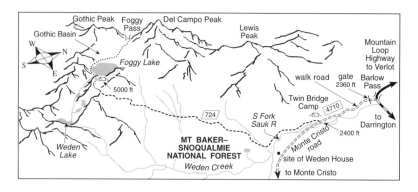

Gothic Basin and Del Campo Peak

creek bed of unstable boulders, mainly in a deep gully. The good news is that the steady steepness forces a rest-stop pace that permits leisure to enjoy the deep forest of old trees. The even better news is that the scene of erosion is passed, the trail remains as tilted as ever, but in a remarkable condition of self-preservation.

At 3500 feet the way emerges from shadows of the ancient forest into sky-airy mountain hemlock and heather. Three streams rush down gorges, big, middling, and small, until early August possibly snow-filled and dangerous. Views open across the gulf of Weden Creek to Silvertip Peak and others above old Monte Cristo town. Flowers begin.

The tread gets skimpy and rocky but, never fear, constantly steep to King Kong's Showerbath, 4100 feet. Hereabouts were the mine head-quarters, naught remaining save rusty metal and rotten wood. The trail to here, mean as it seemed in the walking, now becomes a golden memory. The rest of the way was beaten out by a later generation of prospectors who were banging rocks as late as 1969 but expending minimal effort on the trail, which has many a slippery pitch. At 4500 feet, however, difficulties pretty well cease in a parkland traverse of the valley wall, past several campsites perched on little terraces, views down and out to peaks. At 4950 feet, some 5 miles from Barlow Pass, voilà, Gothic La, doorway of the basin. Let the wandering begin! To fishless Foggy (Crater) Lake in a solemn cirque at 5200 feet. To Foggy Pass, 5500 feet, between Gothic and Del Campo Peaks.

Good campsites are scattered through the basin. Please, no wood fires (most of the wood was burnt up long ago anyhow).

28 SILVER LAKE–TWIN LAKES

**Round trip from Barlow Pass to
Silver Lake 11 miles**
Hiking time 8 hours
High point 4350 feet
Elevation gain 2000 feet

**Round trip to Twin Lakes 17
miles**
Hiking time 12 hours
High point 5400 feet
**Elevation gain 3500 feet in, 1000
feet out**

Hikable July through October
Backpack
Map: Green Trails No. 143 Monte Cristo
**Current information: Ask at Darrington Ranger Station about trail
Nos. 708 and 708A**

Three beautiful lakes, especially lovely in fall colors. The nearest
and easiest, Silver Lake, is tucked in a cirque of cliffs, waterfalls, and
meadows. Twin Lakes, 3 grueling miles farther, are twin pools of deep
blue beneath the great east face of Columbia Peak.

The authors don't want to hear any hikers whimpering about the December 26, 1980, flood that ripped up the road to Monte Cristo and
forced them to walk 4 extra miles, each way. The Christmas flood was
the best thing that's happened to this valley since the railroad shut
down. The 4 miles now free of automobiles are the most scenic valley
walk, forest walk, river walk in the area, with many excellent back-
packer campsites, a terrific place to introduce little children to a life
away from automobiles. Further, those 4 miles multiplied by 2 convert
certain former day walks amid crowds to lonesome wildland backpacks.

Drive the Mountain Loop Highway about 20 miles from the Verlot
Public Service Center to Barlow Pass and park near the gated Monte
Cristo road, elevation 2360 feet.

Hike the Monte Cristo road 4 delightful miles to a junction. The left
is to a campground. Take the right toward the Monte Cristo townsite,
cross the Sauk River, and in a few feet reach the trailhead, elevation
2753 feet, signed "Silver Lake."

The trail is steep, eroded by water and boots, and cluttered by boulders, giant roots, and stumps from clearcutting on private property, so
though it's only 1½ miles to Silver Lake, expect to spend 2 hours getting there. At 4350 feet the way crosses Poodle Dog Pass. Here the Silver Lake and the Twin Lakes trails separate.

For Silver Lake, go right from the pass ¼ mile to the shore, 4260
feet. Camping is permitted, but no fires; bring a stove. For the best
views and picnics cross the outlet and climb open slopes 700 feet to a
shoulder of Silvertip Peak. Look down Silver Creek toward Mineral
City and beyond Silver Lake to the Monte Cristo peaks. In season,
graze blue fruit.

For Twin Lakes, go left on a boot-beaten track that follows an old
miners' trail. The way is strenuous and rugged, gaining (and partly

losing) 1500 feet in the 2½ miles to a viewpoint 650 feet above the lakes. Though the route is well defined it would be easy to lose in snow, so don't go before August. In the first mile the up-down trail rounds a ridge with views out Silver Creek to logging roads. After dropping to pass under a cliff, at about 2 miles it climbs to a viewpoint over the deep hole of Seventysix Gulch to Wilmon Spires.

Walk on—and scramble along, above cliffs—the ridge crest. Some 150 feet before the highest point of the ridge, the trail contours right toward an obvious pass and at 2½ miles reaches the lakes view, elevation 5400 feet, far enough for most hikers. Make a wrong turn here and you're in cliffs. To reach the lakes go right, descending to the obvious pass and then following the trail down a wide terrace to the lakes. Campsites are plentiful; no fires.

Silvertip Peak and Twin Lakes trail

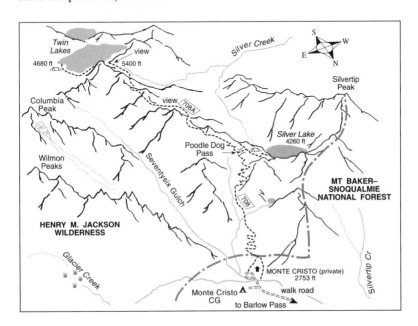

29 GLACIER BASIN

Round trip from Barlow Pass
  13½ miles
Allow 2 days
High point 4500 feet
Elevation gain 2200 feet
Hikable July through October

Map: Green Trails No. 143 Monte
  Cristo
Current information: Ask at Dar-
  rington Ranger Station about
  trail No. 719

Meadows and boulders, flowers and snowfields, cold streams for wading and soft grass for napping, all in a dream basin tucked amid fierce peaks.

Until the flood of December 26, 1980, this was so short and popular a hike any observer could plainly see the eventual total devastation of the scene. The only salvation in sight was that popularity was generating unpopularity. Now the hike is long—too long for a rational day or even a relaxed weekend—and more glorious than it's been since the 1940s, when the automobile poked its nose into this valley. It would be a mad, mad world that reopened the road to Monte Cristo and thus rejected Mother Nature's gift.

Drive the Mountain Loop Highway some 20 miles from the Verlot Public Service Center to Barlow Pass and park near the gated Monte Cristo road, elevation 2360 feet.

Walk the road 4⅓ miles, noting the many excellent spots to camp by the river. Introduce children to wilderness or basecamp for day hikes to high country. At 4½ miles the road splits, the left fork to a campground; go right, on the main drag through Monte Cristo, past the sites of hotel sites, the brothels, and the saloons. The road-trail continues 1 more mile to the end, now a scenic campsite.

The "true" trail commences at a moderate grade in open greenery but quickly plunges into Sitka alder and Alaska cedar and tilts straight up. Stop for a rest on a rock outcrop above a magnificent waterfall before tackling the next stretch, the worst, in sunny summertime blisteringly hot and fly-bedeviled. The "trail" is so eroded by years

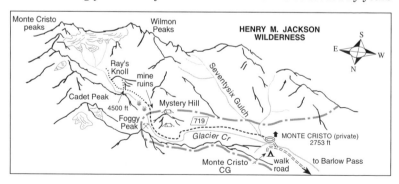

of snowmelt and boots that, were it not for the alder handholds, the rock slabs and mud walls would require mountaineering equipment. Going up, think how bad it's going to be coming *down*. But there's only ½ mile of the worst (an hour up, an hour down). The track then eases out in a gulch filled with talus, snow, and whistling marmots.

The difficulties are not quite over. When the water is high the trail is flooded and hikers must scramble over boulders. At 4500 feet, 2½ miles from Monte Cristo townsite, with startling abruptness the way opens into the basin—the meandering creeks, the flat fields of grass and blossoms, and the cliffs and glaciers of Cadet and Monte Cristo and Wilmon Peaks, the sharp thrust of Wilmon Spires.

What to do now? Sit and look, have lunch, watch the dippers. Or roam among boulders and wade sandy creeks and maybe organize a snowball fight. Or climb scree slopes to explore old mines. Or take a loitering walk to Ray's Knoll (named for climber Ray Rigg) and views over the basin and down the valley. Scramblers can continue up an easy gully to a higher cirque with glaciers, moraines, waterfalls, and broader views.

But please be kind to the basin meadows. Walk softly. And camp not in the flower fields but on a flat area partway up tree-covered Mystery Hill, to the right as you enter the basin. No fires within ¼ mile of the trail!

Glacier Basin

30   GOAT FLATS

Round trip 9½ miles
Hiking time 6 hours
High point 4700 feet
Elevation gain 2000 feet
Hikable late July through October
One day or backpack

Maps: Green Trails No. 109
   Granite Falls and No. 110
   Silverton
Current information: Ask at Dar-
   rington Ranger Station about
   trail No. 641

The rock spires and icefields of Three Fingers Mountain stand near the west edge of the North Cascades, rising above lowlands and saltwater (the Whulge, to use the name given it by the original residents), prominent on the skyline from as far away as Seattle. On a ridge of the mountain are the lovely alpine meadows of Goat Flats, the most beautiful in the Verlot area. Once upon a time a great network of trails linked the North and South Forks of the Stillaguamish River. Now most of the forest land is chopped up by logging roads, the trails ruined or abandoned or neglected. The hike to Goat Flats follows a small remnant of the old pedestrian network.

Drive the Mountain Loop Highway 7 miles east from Granite Falls and go left on paved Forest Service road No. 41 signed "Tupso Pass." At 0.8 mile pavement ends at a junction; keep left, passing several less-used sideroads. At 11 miles pass the Meadow Mountain trail (an alternate but longer route). At 16.7 miles the road becomes No. (4100)025. At 17.3 miles find the trailhead, elevation 2900 feet.

Trail No. 641 is a classic example of how tread can be completely worn out by the combined efforts of hiking feet and running water. The 2½ miles to Saddle Lake are all roots and rocks and gullies, such slow walking that to do them in less than 2 hours is to risk twisted ankles and broken legs. But take the better with the bitter; improving the trail would increase hiker traffic at Goat Flats, already severely overused. So walk carefully, slowly, blessing the roots and rocks and gullies or at least stifling your curses.

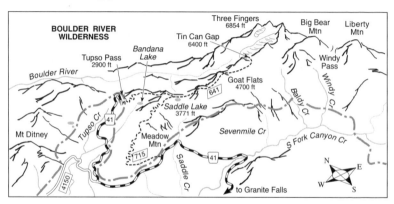

Goat Flats

Just across the outlet of 3771-foot Saddle Lake is a junction with the Meadow Mountain trail and campsites. Go left for Three Fingers and Goat Flats, ascending steep slopes in forests to rolling meadows, acres and acres of blueberries and heather, broken by groves of subalpine trees and dotted with ponds—one in particular, several hundred feet below the trail, offers an excellent camp.

Some 2¼ miles from Saddle Lake the trail enters the meadow plateau of 4700-foot Goat Flats. Near the center is an historic artifact, anciently a log patrol cabin, now just a pile of wood. The meadows are paying the price of beauty, suffering badly from trampling. Visitors will want to leave the trail to pick blueberries and seek viewpoints but, as much as possible, should keep to beaten paths. Camping would better be done along the ridge before the flats; if here, it should be at existing sites. Fires are prohibited everywhere along the ridge.

For most hikers the flats are far enough, offering a close-up view of the cliffs and ice of Three Fingers, looks south to Pilchuck, north to Whitehorse and Mt. Baker, west to the Whulge and the Olympics. Campers get the best: sunsets on peaks and valleys, farm and city lights in the far-below lowland night, a perspective on megalopolis and wildness.

For hikers who want more, the trail goes on, traversing meadows and then climbing steeply up a rocky basin to 6400-foot Tin Can Gap, overlooking what the USGS calls the Queest-Alb Glacier (wherever that name came from). From here a climbers' route drops on steep snow to the glacier, returns to the ridge, and ascends to the base of the pinnacle of the 6854-foot South Peak of Three Fingers, atop which is perched a lookout cabin built in the 1930s. The pinnacle is mounted by a series of ladders. In order to build the cabin the Forest Service dynamited a platform on the summit; tradition says the original summit never was climbed before it was destroyed. Tradition also says one lookout was so stricken by vertigo he had to telephone Forest Service supervisors to come help him down the ladders. Hikers will not want to go beyond Tin Can Gap.

31 MOUNT PILCHUCK

Round trip 4 miles
Hiking time 4 hours
High point 5340 feet
Elevation gain 2400 feet
Hikable July to early November
One day

Map: Green Trails No. 109 Granite
  Falls
Current information: Ask at Darrington Ranger Station about
  trail No. 700

A peak on the exact west edge of the range, prominent on the mountain horizon seen from the lowlands, offering broad views west over
farms, towns, cities, and Whulge (as the original residents called the
saltwater), to the Olympics and views east to the Cascades from Baker
to Rainier. Another prize for those that make the top: in 1989 the
Everett Mountaineers restored the historic lookout cabin and established a museum.

Though the trail is simple and safe, an alarming number of hikers
stray away and stumble or tumble and must be rescued. When the fog
rolls in, or the trail is covered by snow, or a "shortcut" dead-ends, the
cliffs await.

Drive the Mountain Loop Highway east 1 mile from the Verlot Public Service Center. Turn right on Mt. Pilchuck road No. 42 for 6.9 miles
to the trailhead, a bit short of the road-end, elevation 3100 feet.

The trail ascends in gorgeous old-growth forest, skirts the edge of a
1977 clearcut, and switchbacks across the top of the ski slopes of the
abandoned tow hill. The trail rounds the base of Little Pilchuck, climbing heather and ice-polished rock slabs to a saddle and a particularly
infamous and insidiously tempting shortcut. The true and proper and
safe trail drops under a cliff and switchbacks ½ mile up southwest
slopes to the summit.

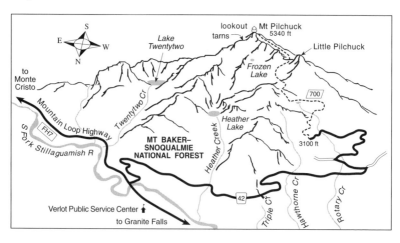

Views from the restored lookout cabin are magnificent—lowland civilization in one direction, mountain wilderness in the other. Immediately below sheer cliffs is Frozen Lake, set in a snowy and rocky cirque. For those with leftover energy, an easy way trail descends 200 feet east along the ridge top to a group of picturesque tarns.

Mount Rainier from Mount Pilchuk

32 BALD MOUNTAIN

One-way trip about 11 miles
Hiking time 6 hours
High point 4500 feet
Elevation gain from
  Stillaguamish 2500 feet, from
  Sultan 2100 feet
Hikable July through October

One day or backpack
Maps: Green Trails No. 110
  Silverton and No. 142 Index
Current information: Ask at Dar-
  rington Ranger Station about
  Bald Mountain Trail

A fine high route traverses the 7-mile ridge separating Sultan Basin and the South Fork Stillaguamish River. Walk the complete way, partly in views of valleys, lakes, and peaks, and partly in deep forest. Or just visit the scenic climax—a dozen small lakes in huckleberry-heather meadows near the summit of 4851-foot Bald Mountain. This climax can be attained from either end or from the Walt Bailey trail (Hike 33).

Stillaguamish start: Drive the Mountain Loop Highway from Granite Falls 4.6 miles past the Verlot Public Service Center and turn right on Schweitzer Creek road No. 4020, signed "Bear Lake Trail" and "Bald Mountain Trail." At 2.3 miles from the highway turn right on road No. 4021, signed "Bald Mountain." In 1.5 miles more go left on road No. (4021)016 for 0.2 mile. At about 4 miles from the Loop Highway reach a large Department of Natural Resources sign and parking lot, elevation 2400 feet.

Walk a road-become-trail a long 1 mile to the veritable trail, which proceeds from old clearcut into old virgin forest, much of the way on puncheon. At ¾ mile pass a sidetrail to Beaver Plant Lake and in a

Three Fingers Mountain from Bald Mountain trail

scant mile reach a Y. The right fork goes a short bit to Upper Ashland Lake and camps. Keep left.

The trail climbs around the end of Bald Ridge in grand forest, at 3 miles topping a 3950-foot saddle with views through the trees of Three Fingers, the Stillaguamish Valley, and Clear Lake, directly below. At about 4 miles the trail, to pass under cliffs, switchbacks down and down 500 feet into the head of the Pilchuck River; here is the first water since the lakes area. The lost elevation is regained and at about 6½ miles is a 4400-foot saddle under the 4851-foot highest peak of Bald Mountain. Here begin those promised meadows.

Sultan start: This end of the trail can be reached from either the town of Sultan or from Granite Falls as described here.

At the second stop sign in Granite Falls, turn right on South Alder Street. At 0.2 mile turn left on East Pioneer Street, signed "Lake Roesiger." At 4.5 miles turn left on DNR road No. 5000 (a large graveled road with a very small road sign). This road has numerous spurs, so when in doubt look carefully for the signs. The road follows the Pilchuck River for miles and then switches from the Pilchuck to the Sultan River watershed. At 17 miles from Granite Falls pass the junction with the road to Sultan, which crosses Culmback Dam.

Stay on road No. 5000 (which may also be marked as Forest Service road No. 6126). The views become spectacular and the road steep. At 24.5 miles from Granite Falls cross Williamson Creek. Drive 1.6 miles farther, then turn left on DNR road No. 6100. Cross Williamson Creek again, and start climbing. At 1.7 miles from Williamson Creek keep left. At 2 miles leave SL-S-6100 and go right. At 2.6 miles reach a junction and the Bald Mountain parking area, elevation about 2400 feet.

Hike the road, switchbacking left, keeping to the right at the first spur and left at the second. At 1 mile the road ends and the foot trail enters forest. At 2 miles the forest becomes more alpine and at 2¾ miles from the parking lot the trail reaches a 4500-foot high point and a junction. The left fork contours around the south side of Bald Mountain 7 miles to Ashland Lakes, as described above; the right fork joins the Walt Bailey trail, which drops a short mile to Cutthroat Lakes, a dozen or more delightful tarns and ponds. Campsites are plentiful, but in late summer running water may be hard to find.

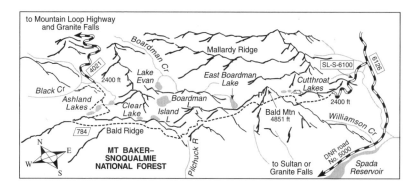

33   WALT BAILEY TRAIL

Round trip 8 miles
Hiking time 5½ hours
High point 4200 feet
Elevation gain 1800 feet
Hikable July to November
One day or backpack

Maps: Green Trails No. 110 Silver-
ton and No. 142 Index (trail not
on maps), USGS Mallardy Ridge
(trail not shown on any map)
Current information: Ask at Dar-
rington Ranger Station about
the Walt Bailey trail

A rough-and-tumble trail to the dozen-odd Cutthroat Lakes scattered about heather-covered meadows on Bald Mountain. For a much easier and shorter trail to Cutthroat Lakes (though a longer drive to the start), see Hike 32.

The trail was constructed entirely by volunteer labor, primarily 73-year-old Walt Bailey and his "young" friends Warren Rush and Ken Countrymen (a former co-worker in the CCC). Lacking trail-building machines and dynamite, the builders had to take the path of least resistance. There thus are many ups and downs to avoid trees, rocky areas, and marshes, and the tread on steep hillsides is skinny. If a Forest Service trail crew had done the job the trail would be wide, with a relatively even grade and little mud. However, it would have cost $200,000, which could be 10 to 15 years in squeezing out of a tight budget.

Grouse

Drive the Mountain Loop Highway past Granite Falls to the Verlot Information Public Service Center and 7 miles beyond. Just short of the Red Bridge, turn right on Mallardy Ridge road No. 4030. At 1.5 miles turn right again on road No. 4032. Avoid sideroads that may look better than the main road and drive to the road-end at 5.7 miles, elevation 3080 feet. Only two or three cars can be parked at the trailhead. More space is 0.3 mile back.

The trail leaves overgrown clearcut for virgin forest, climbing steadily, steeply at times. At about 1 mile it drops a bit, crosses a small creek, and starts up again, often in bogs, to a 3680-foot high point of small heather and blueberry glades. The way drops 200 feet to a lovely meadow

One of the Cutthroat Lakes

at 1¾ miles and continues another 200 feet to pass under a cliff, crosses a rockslide, and starts up—and down—and up some more. About 4 miles from the road is the first of the Cutthroat Lakes, 4200 feet. Others beyond, some with campsites having metal fire rings and toilets.

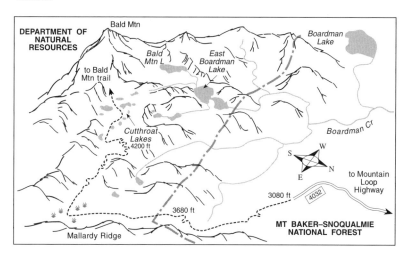

34 WHAT VERLOT FORGOT

Current information: Ask at Darrington Ranger Station

Until the decades after World War II a trail network of some 50-odd miles radiated from the South Fork Stillaguamish River—Canyon Creek, Coal Creek, Bear Creek, Boardman Lakes, Mallardy Ridge, Granite Pass, and Everett's Boy Scout camp at Kelcema Lake. Logging roads obliterated many miles. More were abandoned when no longer needed by forest patrolmen or by the miners (prospectors) who built many of them. Less than half the near-Verlot mileage remains intact. A curious person might ask why this is so, considering that the crowds swarming on the "official" trails of the Verlot vicinity make them so overcrowded that a person pausing to sniff a flower is liable to get trampled.

Are you in a mood to be peaceful and quiet? Try the three abandoned trails noted here. Solitude is 99.9 percent guaranteed.

Mallardy Ridge

Round trip 5 miles	Hikable June through October
Hiking time 6 hours	One day
High point 3800 feet	Map: USGS Mallardy Ridge
Elevation gain 1500 feet	

Of a 14-mile loop that started and ended at the river, 2½ miles along the top of Mallardy Ridge survive.

Drive the Mountain Loop Highway east 7.1 miles from the Verlot Public Service Center. Turn right on road No. 4030 for 6 miles to unmarked trail No. 705, located just where the road swings through a gap in the ridge, elevation 2800 feet.

Wiped out in places by clearcuts and never reestablished, the trail is easy to lose. If you do, go back and find it. It is extremely important to stay on the correct track (the correct ridge!). After the final clearcut the way becomes surprisingly free of blowdowns, easy to walk, following ups and downs of the crest. Climb off the trail to high points to see Sperry and Vesper Peaks and the red-rock south wall of Big Four Mountain.

Marten Creek

Round trip 5 miles	Hikable June through October
Hiking time 4 hours	One day
High point 2800 feet	Map: USGS Silverton (trail not
Elevation gain 1400 feet	shown)

This surviving stretch of the old Granite Pass trail, which crossed to join the Kelcema Lake–Deer Pass trail, is a delightful walk through tall trees. The peaks tower. So does the brush!

Drive east 9.3 miles from the Verlot Public Service Center. A few feet beyond the Marten Creek bridge, find Marten Creek trail No. 713, elevation 1415 feet.

The first mile is on an abandoned, extremely steep mining road. At 1½ miles the trees thin and brush fills the gaps. Salmonberry, thimbleberry, devils club, and vine maple grow waist high, shoulder high, and over your head. At about 2½ miles a small campsite beside Marten Creek is a good turnaround. The old mine apparently was across the creek, its secrets now guarded by jungle. At the valley head, Three Fingers Mountain can be seen poking its head over Granite Pass.

Marble Gulch

Round trip 6 miles	**Hikable June through September**
Hiking time 4 hours	**One day**
High point 4200 feet	**Map: USGS Silverton (trail not**
Elevation gain 1700 feet	**shown)**

A tramway once carried ore from a mine at the headwaters of Williamson Creek up to and over Marble Pass and down to the Stillaguamish. The miners' trail began at Silverton and switchbacked under the tram to the pass, then proceeded 10 miles down to the Sultan River. Private property has blocked access from Silverton; a hiker therefore must wade the Stillaguamish River, only safely possible in late summer.

Drive the Mountain Loop Highway to within 1 mile of Silverton and find a suitable place to ford. On the far side scout around for the trail on the east side (left) of Marble Creek. Only bits and pieces of the original tread survive, but the route is walkable. The best views are a short way up the ridge above the pass.

Sperry and Vesper Peaks and the summit ridge of Big Four Mountain from Mallardy Ridge

35

NORTH LAKE

Round trip 7 miles
Hiking time 6 hours
High point 5070 feet
Elevation gain 1500 feet in,
900 feet out
Hikable mid-July through
September

Map: Green Trails No. 110
Silverton
Current information: Ask at Dar-
rington Ranger Station about
trail No. 712

A steep and at spots difficult trail to heather meadows, tarns, and a lake surrounded by forest, flowers, and cliffs. No wilderness protection means no wilderness restrictions, which may or may not enhance the wildland experience.

Drive the Mountain Loop Highway 15 miles past the Verlot Public Service Center and just short of the Perry Creek bridge turn left on Coal Lake road No. 4060 and drive the 4.7 miles to its end at Independence–North Lake trail No. 712, elevation 3700 feet.

A start on excellent tread soon deteriorates to huge tripping roots and shin-barking rocks. A loss of about 200 feet is made up and then some in the 1 mile or so to Independence Lake, 3720 feet. Round the left shore to campsites at the inlet. Select from the confusion of paths the North Lake trail, which switchbacks up steep slopes to the right, mostly on tread almost lost in brush and flowers, and in several places altogether vanishes, requiring stretches of scrambling. Elevation is gained relentlessly, 1300 feet in 1½ miles. A huge Alaskan cedar with twin tops, if considered a single tree, must be a record holder. Across the valley is red-topped Devils Thumb.

The way eventually drops a bit, crosses a small meadow, and climbs to a divide overlooking Murphy Creek. Viewpoint paths go this way

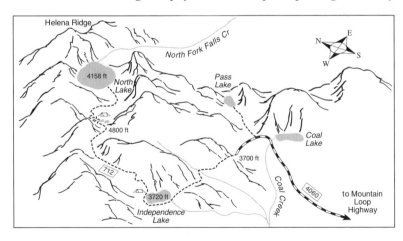

North Lake

and that. Keep right and at 4800 feet enter heather meadows, with two small tarns, one large enough to provide good camping. Another 200-foot climb tops a saddle overlooking the North Fork Falls Creek valley. A bit farther is a view down to North Lake, some 700 feet below. The trail works its way through the heather over, around, and under glacier-scoured cliffs and past small tarns and then descends to the lakeshore, 4158 feet, 3½ miles from the road. Camping at the lake is very limited. The best places are near the tarns. About 100 yards before arriving at the lake on the left-hand side of the trail is a toilet.

36 PERRY CREEK– MOUNT FORGOTTEN

Round trip to meadows 8 miles
Hiking time 7 hours
High point 5200 feet
Elevation gain 3100 feet
**Hikable mid-June through
  October**

One day or backpack
**Map: Green Trails No. 111 Sloan
  Peak**
**Current information: Ask at Dar-
  rington Ranger Station about
  trail No. 711**

A valley forest famed for its botanical richness, a waterfall, a small alpine meadow, and views of the impressive wall of Big Four Mountain and the white volcano of Glacier Peak. Come early for flowers, come late for blueberries.

Drive the Mountain Loop Highway east 15.5 miles from the Verlot Public Service Center. Just after crossing Perry Creek turn left on Perry Creek road No. 4063 for 1 mile to the road-end, elevation 2100 feet.

The trail traverses a steep hillside, now in forest, now in a grand display of ferns and flowers, boulder-hops a frenzied creek, and at 2 miles climbs above Perry Creek Falls. Pause to look over the top of the falls—but don't trust the handrail. A few feet farther the way crosses Perry Creek on boulders. A campsite is here.

Elevation is gained steadily in old-growth timber, which at 3½ miles yields to a field of heather and lupine dotted by subalpine trees. The trail switchbacks up forests on the slopes of Mt. Forgotten. Near the top of the switchbacks an abandoned trail branches off left, contouring then climbing ½ mile to the ridge top near Stillaguamish Peak and ending on a cliff above South Lake. The main trail goes right, enters lush, fragile meadows, and disappears at about 5200 feet, 4 miles.

Novice hikers should turn back here, well rewarded by views of Glacier Peak, seen at the head of the long valley of the White Chuck River,

Small tarn at end of trail

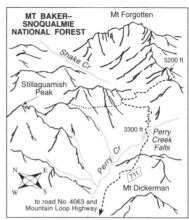

Perry Creek Falls

and closer views of Big Four, Twin Peaks, Mt. Dickerman, and the long ridge of Stillaguamish Peak.

Experienced off-trail travelers can continue onward and upward a mile, climbing very steep heather slopes, then scrambling broken rock, to the 6005-foot summit of the peak and more views.

37   MOUNT DICKERMAN

Round trip 8½ miles
Hiking time 8–9 hours
High point 5723 feet
Elevation gain 3900 feet
Hikable late July through
   October

One day
Map: Green Trails No. 111 Sloan
   Peak
Current information: Ask at Dar-
   rington Ranger Station about
   trail No. 710

All too few trails remain, outside wilderness areas and national parks, that begin in valley bottoms and climb unmarred forests to meadows. The way to Dickerman is strenuous, but the complete expe-

rience of life zones from low to high, plus the summit views, are worth every drop of sweat.

Drive the Mountain Loop Highway east 16.6 miles from the Verlot Public Service Center to about 2.5 miles beyond Big Four Picnic Area, to a small parking area and easily overlooked trail sign, elevation 1900 feet.

Trail No. 710 doesn't fool around. Switchbacks commence instantly climbing up and up and up through lovely cool forest; except perhaps in late summer, several small creeks provide pauses that refresh. Tantalizing glimpses through timber give promise of scenery above. A bit past 2 miles lower-elevation trees yield to Alaska cedars and subalpine firs. Then the forest thins as the trail traverses under towering cliffs onto flatter terrain. Near here, in a sheltered hollow to the west, is a snowmelt lakelet reached by a faint path; camping is possible.

The next ½ mile ranks among the most famous blueberry patches in the Cascades; in season, grazing hikers may find progress very slow indeed. In the fall, photographers find the blazing colors equally obstructive. Now, too, the horizons grow.

The final mile is somewhat steeper, switchbacking meadows to the broad summit, as friendly a sackout spot as one can find. Abrupt cliffs drop toward Perry Creek forests, far below. Beyond are Stillaguamish Peak and Mt. Forgotten. To the east rise Glacier Peak, the horn of Sloan Peak, and all the Monte Cristo peaks. Across the South Fork Stillaguamish River are rugged Big Four Mountain and the striking rock slabs of Vesper Peak.

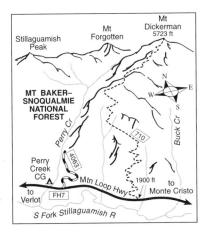

Three Fingers Mountain from Mount Dickerman

38 SUNRISE MINE TRAIL– HEADLEE PASS

Round trip 5 miles
Hiking time 5 hours
High point 4600 feet
Elevation gain 2500 feet
Hikable August and September
One day

Map: Green Trails No. 111 Sloan Peak
Current information: Ask at Darrington Ranger Station about trail No. 707

Theirs not to reason why, Theirs but to do and die: Into the valley of Death rode the six hundred.

Judging by the avalanche debris, the narrow valley ascended by the Sunrise Mine trail must be bombarded by snow, rock, and broken trees from the first snowfall in October until all the snow has slid from surrounding peaks sometime after mid-July. Hikers may feel they *are* the Light Brigade as they trudge into the valley, but if they make sure not to do so until the heavy artillery has ceased for the summer, the risk is no greater than on any other steep, rough, and often snow-covered terrain. The happy demise of the Monte Cristo road has put that area's several popular trails much deeper in de facto wilderness, glory be; as a consequence, more and more hikers with limited time have been finding the Sunrise Mine Trail on their own. Best that they (you) be warned what to expect.

Drive the Mountain Loop Highway east 17.8 miles from the Verlot Public Service Center toward (not to) Barlow Pass. Turn right on Sunrise Mine road No. 4065 for 2.3 miles to the road-end and trailhead, elevation 2100 feet. (The final 0.5 mile often is blocked by a slide.)

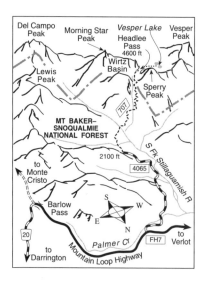

In the first ½ mile through forest the root-and-rock trail crosses four creeks, including—on a slippery log—the incipient South Fork Stillaguamish River. The second ½ mile, still rough, switchbacks steeply up a fern-covered hillside, rounds a corner, and levels briefly as the trail enters the steep, narrow valley of death or whatever.

Avalanche fans may remain unmelted all summer, or even for years. Just because you're technically "on" a trail don't be silly about steep, hard snow. Unless the way is clear, be satisfied with the valley view of peaks piercing the sky.

The miners who built the trail

Headlee Pass trail

begrudged time that could be spent more entertainingly digging holes in the ground and sought to gain maximum elevation with minimum distance. No fancy-Dan 10-percent grade for *them*—the final mile, gaining 1200 feet to Headlee Pass, is 15 to 20 percent, ideal for hikers who also have no time to waste. The last 500 feet is in a slot gully where the grade has to be remade every summer by unpaid volunteers.

Headlee Pass, 4600 feet, is a thin cut in the ridge with rather limited views, confined by cliffs on three sides and snowy Vesper Peak to the west. The trail continues a short distance beyond the pass to an end at the edge of a giant rockslide; at one time it went to Sunrise Mine. A faint way trail crosses the slide to tiny Vesper Lake, often snowbound even on Labor Day.

39 SULTAN BASIN DNR TRAILS

Map: Green Trails No. 142 Index

Due to faulty mathematics when it entered the Union in 1889, Washington failed to obtain the full land grant due from the federal government. The error belatedly was noticed and the U.S. Forest Service handed over a large tract in the Mt. Pilchuck–Sultan River area. Even more belatedly, the state Department of Natural Resources commenced providing Forest Service–style recreational opportunities. Among the fruits of the new policy are two superb trails in the Sultan Basin leading to lovely subalpine lakes.

Drive US 2 to Sultan and on the east side of town, near the top of the hill, turn left on a road signed "Sultan Basin Recreation Area." From the west, the sign is obscured and there is no turn lane; if you are unable to get off the highway—safely—on the first pass, try again, cautiously.

Drive the Sultan Basin road 13 miles to Olney Pass, entry to the Everett Watershed. Visitors must register here. Car camping is forbidden in the watershed but trail camping is allowed from June 15 through October 15. However, be certain to use the toilet facilities so authorities will have no reason to prohibit backpackers.

Proceed a few feet from the pass to a three-way junction. Take the

Big Greider Lake

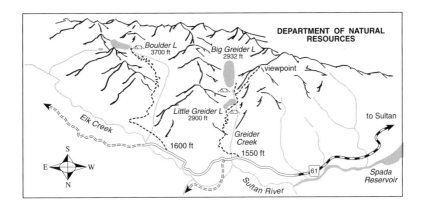

middle road, No. 61, and drive 7 miles to the Greider Lakes trailhead or 8.3 miles to the Boulder Lake trailhead.

Greider Lakes

Round trip 5 miles
Hiking time 3 hours
High point 2932 feet

Elevation gain 1350 feet
Hikable June through November
One day or backpack

Two delightful cirque lakes ringed by cliffs. There are excellent campsites at both.

Find the trail in a large parking area, elevation about 1550 feet. The path immediately enters forest, passes a picnic area and nature trail, and then starts switchbacking up a very steep hillside. The tread is rough with boulders, roots, and even some short stairways, which are not easy for short-legged people. At 2 miles, 2900 feet, reach Little Greider Lake and campsites. Cross the outlet stream and continue another ½ mile to Big Greider Lake and more campsites. Toilets at both lakes.

For greater views, go right near Big Greider Lake, climbing 600 feet in ¾ mile to a dramatic viewpoint.

Boulder Lake

Round trip 8 miles
Hiking time 5 hours
High point 3700 feet

Elevation gain 2100 feet
Hikable July through October
One day or backpack

The boulders are on the far side of the lake. The near side—the trail side—is meadows and forests and excellent campsites.

The trailhead, elevation 1600 feet, is on a badly eroded old logging road, which for 1 mile, gaining 800 feet, is now trail. The angle moderates on true though rough trail across a brushy rockslide to forest at 1½ miles. The tread improves as switchbacks to a steep sidehill marsh at 3 miles, traversed on puncheon. At 4 miles is the lake, 3700 feet.

The camps are across the outlet stream on a heather slope. Toilets are atop the knoll. Thick brush along the shores prevents an easy walk to the far-side boulders.

40   BLANCA LAKE

Round trip 8 miles
Hiking time 6–8 hours
High point 4600 feet
Elevation gain 2700 feet in,
  600 feet out
Hikable July through October

One day or backpack
Map: Green Trails No. 143
  Monte Cristo
Current information: Ask at Sky-
  komish Ranger Station about
  trail No. 1052

The rugged cliffs of Kyes, Monte Cristo, and Columbia Peaks above, the white mass of the Columbia Glacier in the upper trough, and the deep waters of ice-fed Blanca Lake filling the lower cirque. A steep forest climb ending in grand views, with further explorations available to the experienced off-trail traveler. This is a popular trip for day-hiking, but camping is too limited and cramped to be recommended.

Drive US 2 to the Index junction and turn left on the North Fork Skykomish River road 15 miles. Just before crossing the North Fork is a four-way junction; turn left 2 miles on road No. 63 to the Blanca Lake trailhead sign and parking area, elevation 1900 feet.

Trail No. 1052 immediately gets down to the business of grinding out elevation, relentlessly switchbacking up and up in forest. At 3 miles the way reaches the ridge top at 4600 feet, the highest point of the trip, and at last enters the Henry M. Jackson Wilderness. In a few hundred yards is shallow little Virgin Lake, amid meadows and trees of a saddle on the very crest. Acceptable camping here for those who don't wish to carry packs farther, but no water in late summer.

Now the trail goes down, deteriorating to a mere route as it sidehills through trees with glimpses of blue-green water, dropping 600 feet in 1 mile and reaching the 3972-foot lake at the outlet. Relax and enjoy the wind-rippled, sun-sparkling lake, ¾ mile long, the Columbia Glacier, the spectacular peaks. Do not camp on the lakeshore. A bench to the right has a site and by crossing the outlet stream and following a boot-beaten path toward the head of the lake several more can be found. No fires permitted; carry a stove.

Experienced hikers can explore the rough west shore to the braided stream channels and waterfalls and flowers at the head of the lake. For a spectacular view

Mountain daisy

Air view of Columbia Glacier, Blanca Lake, and Kyes Peak

of lake and mountains, hike to the top of 5128-foot Toil Peak, the first of two wooded bumps between Virgin Lake and Troublesome Mountain. On the highest point of the trail above Virgin Lake find a faint path traversing heather meadows southward, climbing at times steeply to the summit.

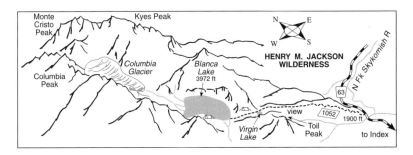

West Cady Ridge

SKYKOMISH RIVER
Henry M. Jackson Wilderness

41 WEST CADY RIDGE SPRINGTIME HIKE

Round trip to viewpoint 8 miles, to Bench Mark Mountain 16 miles
One day
High point 4761 feet
Elevation gain 2200 feet to viewpoint

Hikable mid-June through September
Maps: Green Trails No. 143 Monte Cristo and No. 144 Benchmark
Current information: Ask at Skykomish Ranger Station about trail No. 1054

The final leg of the 24-mile Dishpan Gap–Bench Mark Loop described in Hikes 42 and 43 is a popular early summer hike through miles of mountain meadows and groves of subalpine firs and mountain hemlocks. If snow permits, go all the way to the site of former Bench Mark Mountain Lookout at 5816 feet.

Drive US 2 to the Index junction and turn left on the North Fork Skykomish River road 15 miles to a four-way junction just before the

North Fork bridge. Go left 4.6 miles on road No. 63, to the West Cady Ridge and Quartz Creek trailheads, elevation 2500 feet.

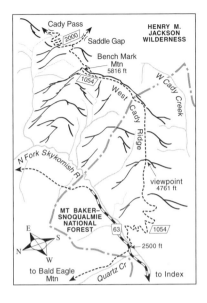

Find West Cady Ridge trail No. 1054 on the south side of the road and head upstream, cross the river on a sturdy bridge, and start climbing virgin forest. Long switchbacks change to short ones as the trail leaves the big trees and ascends the spine of a narrow ridge to a saddle at 3600 feet. The trail gains another 600 feet on a broad ridge crest, through fields of waist-high huckleberries (grazing begins in late August). The views already are sensational, but don't give up yet. At about 4 miles from the car is a heathery 4761-foot high point in views north to Columbia and Kyes Peaks, northeast to Glacier Peak, and west to Jacks Pass and rugged peaks of the Eagle Rock Roadless Area. Enjoy, for an hour or a whole day.

But the fun has only begun. The trail follows the ridge crest eastward 4 more miles, of meadows and forest, each high point adding more views climaxing on 5816-foot Bench Mark Mountain.

Blueberry time in late summer

42 NORTH FORK– BENCH MARK LOOP

Long loop trip 23½ miles
Allow 2–3 days
High point 5816 feet
Elevation gain 4700 feet
Hikable mid-July through late
September

Maps: Green Trails No. 143 Monte
Cristo and No. 144
Current information: Ask at Skykomish Ranger Station about
trail Nos. 1051, 1053, 1054, and
2000

A loop through miles of forest and meadow flowers, starting on the North Fork Skykomish River trail and climbing to the Pacific Crest Trail. A 1½-mile road walk connects the beginning and end; if transportation can be arranged between the two trailheads, subtract 1½ miles and 500 feet of elevation gain from the trip log. A shorter loop of 17 miles used to be our favorite North Fork hike but the loss of two bridges has made it difficult if not downright suicidal much of the summer.

Except for West Cady Ridge, the route offers good campsites all along the way; camp the first night 4 or 5 miles up the trail and the second night on the Crest Trail near Pass Creek.

Drive US 2 to Index junction and turn left on the North Fork Skykomish River road 15 miles. Just before the North Fork bridge, at a four-way junction, go left 6 miles on road No. 63, pass the West Cady Ridge (Hike 41) and Quartz Creek trailheads, and continue to the road-end and the North Fork Skykomish trailhead, elevation 3000 feet. If doing a loop, unload packs here and drive back 1.4 miles to where the loop will end at West Cady Ridge trailhead. Leave the car here and walk back up the road.

Hike 1½ miles on North Fork trail No. 1051 to the junction with Pass Creek trail No. 1053, signed "Cady Pass 3½ miles," elevation 3200 feet. This is the start of the shorter 17-mile loop with the difficult all-summer river crossing.

From the Pass Creek junction continue on the North Fork trail, the tread sometimes excellent and sometimes poor. At about 4 miles from

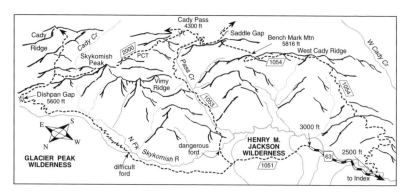

Mount Rainier from Bench Mark Mountain

the road is a boulder-hopping ford of the North Fork Skykomish River (which may be hazardous in high water) to a nice campsite. At 5 miles the path traverses a large huckleberry parkland, the camp commodious and well watered. The way then climbs to Dishpan Gap and the Pacific Crest Trail, 5600 feet, 7½ miles from the road.

Head south on the Crest Trail (Hike 60) 4 miles through beautiful alpine meadows, passing Wards Pass and Lake Sally Ann to Cady Pass; ½ mile beyond the pass is the end of the Pass Creek trail, 4200 feet.

Continue south on the Crest Trail 2¼ miles and go right on West Cady Ridge trail No. 1054, 4900 feet. In a short distance is a steep snowbank that may not melt out until late July. Above the snow make the short sidetrip to take in the highest point of the ridge, 5816-foot Bench Mark Mountain, with fields of heather and flowers and horizons of views, including Sloan Peak, the Monte Cristo peaks, Glacier, Baker, and Rainier.

Now begins a delightful walk in alpine meadows and forest as the way follows the ups and downs of 4-mile-long West Cady Ridge. From the abrupt end the trail descends a series of short switchbacks at 8 miles from the Crest Trail reaching the North Fork Skykomish River road.

43 THE GRAND DISHPAN GAP LOOP

Loop trip 31 miles
Allow 3 days
High point 5800 feet
Elevation gain 5200 feet
Hikable July through September

Map: Green Trails No. 144
   Benchmark
Current information: Ask at Sky-
   komish Ranger Station about
   trail Nos. 1050, 650, 2000, and
   1054

Dishpan Gap is treated on four trips in this book—and justly so, considering the flower fields, views, and campsites. This loop is longer but has no problems with early-season river crossings, no shuffling cars, just miles and miles of ridgetop roaming. However, snowbanks can be a problem, even in late summer.

Drive the North Fork Skykomish River road No. 63 (Hike 41) 4.6

Pride Basin from Bald Eagle Mountain

miles to the Quartz Creek and West Cady Ridge trailheads, elevation 2500 feet.

The first leg of this loop follows Quartz Creek trail No. 1050 in woods 4½ miles to Curry Gap. Turn right there on trail No. 650 toward Bald Eagle Mountain (Hike 23) and climb into ridgetop meadows. In 8½ up and down miles is a junction. The left fork drops to the two Blue Lakes and camping. Go straight ahead 3 miles to Dishpan Gap and the Pacific Crest Trail at 5600 feet, about 16 miles from the road.

The second leg heads south 4 miles on the Pacific Crest Trail (Hikes 42 and 60), through flower-bright meadows past Wards Pass and Lake Sally Ann, and down into the timber of 4300-foot Cady Pass. From there the Crest Trail switchbacks in meadows toward Saddle Gap.

A few feet shy of the gap go right on West Cady Ridge trail No. 1054 (Hike 41) 9 miles back to the starting point.

Clark's nutcracker

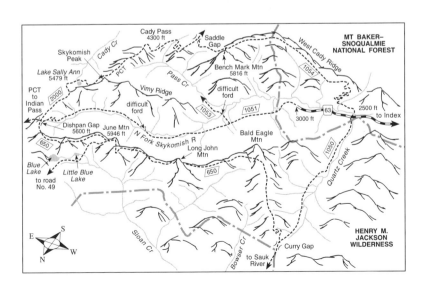

44 BARCLAY AND EAGLE LAKES

Round trip to Eagle Lake 8½ miles
Hiking time 6 hours
High point 3888 feet
Elevation gain 1700 feet
Hikable late June through October

One day or backpack
Map: Green Trails No. 143 Monte Cristo
Current information: Ask at Skykomish Ranger Station about trail No. 1055

For many years Barclay Lake was among the most popular low-elevation hikes in the Cascades, passing through pleasant old forest to the base of the tremendous north wall of Mt. Baring, a good trip in early spring and late fall when higher country was deep in snow. The wall remains, and the lake, but not much forest. Tragically, the walk to Barclay Lake no longer deserves, by itself, inclusion in this book. However, there is still Eagle Lake, amid trees, meadows, and peaks, and offering a staggering cross-valley look at the north wall of Baring, a legend among climbers and, to date, ascended only once.

Drive US 2 some 6 miles east from the Index junction. Turn left at Baring on 635 Place NE, cross railroad tracks, and go 4.3 miles on road No. 6024 to the trailhead, elevation 2200 feet.

The trail, with minor ups and downs and numerous mudholes, meanders through what remains of the forest of Barclay Creek, in 1½ miles reaching Barclay Lake, 2422 feet, and at 2¼ miles ending near the inlet stream. Camping is possible at several spots along the shore. Enjoy the neck-stretching look up and up the precipice of 6123-foot Baring Mountain.

At the lakehead, just where the trail leaves the water by a small campsite, find a meager unsigned path climbing 1000 feet straight up steep forest. For a bit the way is on rockslide, then briefly levels and resumes climbing beside another rockslide. The grade abruptly flattens at a viewpoint above Stone Lake and contours to 3888-foot Eagle

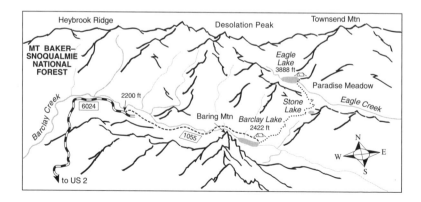

Baring Mountain from Paradise Lakes trail

Lake. By the shore is a cabin, kept locked. For more views, and for meadows, an experienced roamer can scramble up the steep slopes of 5936-foot Townsend Mountain.

Now then. As you are sitting in Paradise Meadow nursing bruises and sprains and wiping sweat from your eyes, you may be hailed by a fisherman who is astounded at your suffering and stupidity, inasmuch as he is just a hour from his car, parked on a logging road up Eagle Creek. And you go home and write a letter demanding to know why this guidebook has put you through this ordeal. Well, what makes it an ordeal is not the steep climb, which enriches the wilderness experience, but learning a road is so near (though not by trail—it's a brush route). Why isn't the road gated, banning public vehicles, and thus placing Eagle Creek back in deep wilderness where it belongs?

45 SCORPION MOUNTAIN

Round trip 9 miles
Hiking time 6 hours
High point 5540 feet
Elevation gain 2300 feet in,
300 feet out
Hikable July through October

One day
Maps: Green Trails No. 143 Monte
Cristo and No. 144 Benchmark
Current information: Ask at Sky-
komish Ranger Station about
trail No. 1067

Looking for views from an easy trail? Looking for a pleasant family walk? Choose any other destination but Scorpion! Even the access road, carved into a steep hillside stripped bare of trees, is difficult. And there is no water on the path, making at least one loaded canteen essential. However, hikers seeking solitude, fields of wildflowers that as soon as the snow melts progress from avalanche lilies to lupine and paintbrush, a nice view—and a good sweat—will find Scorpion just their cup of tea.

Avalanche lily

Drive US 2 to Skykomish. Just 0.2 mile beyond town turn left on Beckler River road No. 65. At 7 miles turn right on road No. 6520, signed (sign missing in 1994) "Johnson Creek" and "Johnson Ridge Trail." At a junction 1.7 miles from the Beckler River road keep straight ahead at a junction and at 5.6 miles turn right on No. 6526 to its end some 7 miles from the Beckler River, elevation 3600 feet. (Don't be confused by a spur road 0.3 mile from the road-end).

Trail No. 1067 begins on ½ mile of abandoned road. Keep left at a switchback, reaching real trail at ¾ mile, on the ridge top. Windfalls obscure the way but detouring around them is no problem. If the seldom-walked tread is lost, just follow the forested ridge top. Openings in the trees occasionally offer glimpses south of rocky 6190-foot Mt. Fernow. At 2¼ miles the trail crosses the top of 5056-foot Sunrise Mountain, with a view of Glacier Peak, and drops about 300 feet before climbing nearly to the top of 5540-foot

Johnson Ridge

Scorpion Mountain at 4 miles. Leave the path at its highest point and ascend the ridge a few hundred feet to the summits' lush carpet of grass and flowers and a grand panorama of the Cascades.

The trail continues around the south shoulder of the mountain and drops 500 feet to tiny Joan Lake at 4½ miles, a popular mosquito rendezvous. Volunteers have partially reopened 5½ miles of an old trail from Scorpion Mountain to Captain Point and Scenic.

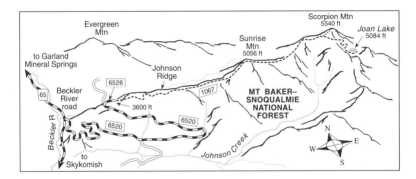

46 A PEACH, A PEAR, AND A TOPPING (MEADOW CREEK TRAIL)

Round trip to Pear Lake 16 miles
Allow 2 days
High point 5200 feet
Elevation gain 3200 feet in,
500 feet out
Hikable July through October

Map: Green Trails No. 144
    Benchmark
Current information: Ask at
    Skykomish Ranger Station
    about trail No. 1057

Savor flower and heather gardens ringing three alpine lakes and a spatter of ponds along the Pacific Crest Trail. And if all these sweet things seem to call for whipped cream, stroll to a peak for the panorama of a horizon full of valleys and mountains.

To approach from the east, drive road No. 6701 from the Little Wenatchee River (Hike 50) and at 4 miles past the junction with road No. (6701)400 find Top Lake trail No. 1506. From the more popular west, drive US 2 to Skykomish and just east of town turn north on Beckler River road No. 65. At 7 miles turn right 4 more miles on Rapid River road No. 6530 to Meadow Creek trail No. 1057, elevation 2100 feet.

Beginning amid the ravages of the 1967 Evergreen Mountain fire and subsequent salvage logging, now a mixture of silver snags and young trees, the trail gains almost 1000 feet switchbacking out of the Rapid River valley. At about 1½ miles the burn is left, forest entered, and the grade moderates and contours into Meadow Creek drainage, crossing Meadow Creek at 3 miles by hopping boulders (there aren't really enough). At 3¾ miles recross the creek and climb steeply from Meadow Creek into the West Cady Creek drainage. At 6½ miles reach the lower of the two Fortune Ponds, 4700 feet, and an intersection with the Pacific Crest Trail.

Walk south on the Crest trail 1¼ miles, cross 5200-foot Frozen Finger Pass between West Cady Creek and the Rapid River, and drop to 4809-foot Pear Lake, 8 miles from the car. Do not camp within 200 feet of the shores here or at Fortune Ponds. The meadows are so fragile, and so damaged, you really ought to sling a hammock in the trees.

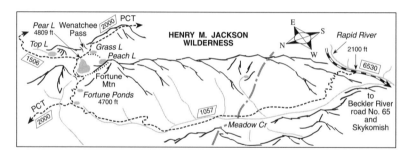

Peach Lake, at the same elevation over the ridge south, is best reached by contouring off-trail around the ridge end and below cliffs, passing narrow Grass Lake. Top Lake is attained via ½ mile more on the Crest Trail and another ½ mile on trail No. 1506. For the promised land of views, leave the trail at Fortune Ponds and ascend Fortune Mountain, 5903 feet.

Upper Fortune Pond

47 SKYKOMISH TRAILS TO BE

In the Eagle Rock, Beckler–Alpine Baldy Ridge, and Windy Mountain Roadless Areas

While National Wilderness trails of the Cascades are overwhelmed, some of the largest and most lonesome alpine meadows and lakes in the Skykomish district lie outside National Wilderness in the Eagle Rock, Beckler–Alpine Baldy Ridge, and Windy Mountain Roadless Areas. Until the 1950s, 50 miles of trail traversed these heather-and-flower ridges. But trails were plentiful and hikers few, so logging roads (to ship trees to Japan) replaced miles of footways and more miles were simply abandoned. Though these roadless areas had all the qualifications required for inclusion in the National Wilderness system, in the lack of trails few knew what was there, and in the absence of vociferous support by hikers, they were excluded from the 1984 Washington Wilderness Bill.

In the 1980s, as the popularity of hiking exploded, crowding the National Wilderness, concerned hikers and Forest Service staff looked at the miles of abandoned trails in roadless areas and realized their great potential. However, the trails had so deteriorated that only bits and pieces of the old tread could be found, most was so lost, and, therefore, reopening means new construction.

Although the Forest Service promised new trails, their priorities for construction favored ORV trails, horse bridges, and wheelchair nature paths; no funds were left over for new hiking trails. It wasn't until 1994 that preliminary surveys for alternative trails in the Eagle Rock and Beckler–Alpine Baldy Roadless Areas were made, construction planned for 1996. Meanwhile, Congress has virtually eliminated trail construction money; it may be another 10 years before the first alternative can be built. Until then, only a person skilled at cross-country travel can hope to find the boot-beaten paths that presently give access

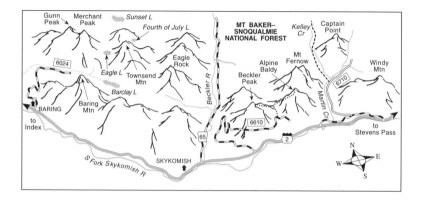

120

Flower fields on side of Captain Point

to the mountain lakes and alpine ridges in the three roadless areas.

Eagle Rock Roadless Area: USGS Baring, Evergreen Mtn.; 28 miles of new trail planned.

Beckler–Alpine Baldy Roadless Area: USGS Captain Point, Scenic, Skykomish; 18 miles of new trail planned and the 4 miles of Kelly Creek to be restored.

Windy Mountain Roadless Area: USGS Scenic and Captain Point; 6 miles of new trail planned.

48 LAKE VALHALLA

Round trip 11 miles
Hiking time 6 hours
High point 5100 feet
Elevation gain 1100 feet in,
400 feet out
Hikable mid-July through
October

One day or backpack
Map: Green Trails No. 144
Benchmark
Current information: Ask at Lake
Wenatchee Ranger Station
about trail No. 2000

North from Stevens Pass the Pacific Crest Trail roams by a succession of meadowy alpine lakes. First in line is Lake Valhalla, set in a cirque under the cliffs of Lichtenberg Mountain.

Lake Valhalla

Drive US 2 to Stevens Pass, elevation 4061 feet, and park in the lot at the east end of the summit area. Find the trail beside the utility substation.

The way begins along the original grade of the Great Northern Railroad, used when trains went over the top of the pass; the right-of-way was abandoned upon completion of the first Cascade Tunnel (predecessor of the present tunnel) early in the century.

From the open hillside, views extend beyond the pass to ski slopes and down Stevens Creek to Nason Creek and far east out the valley. Below is the roar of highway traffic. In 1½ miles the gentle path rounds the end of the ridge and enters the drainage of Nason Creek.

The main trail descends a bit to cross a small stream, climbs a ridge, and at 3½ miles enters a basin of meadows and marsh, with a fine campsite. Staying east and below the Cascade Crest, the way ascends easily to a 5100-foot spur, then drops to the rocky shore of the 4830-foot lake.

Heavily used and frequently crowded camps lie among the trees near the inlet. The best sites are near the outlet, where the terrain is less fragile. No fires are permitted, of course; carry a stove. For explorations climb heather meadows to the summit of 5844-foot Lichtenberg and broad views or continue north on the Pacific Crest Trail (Hike 100) as far as time and energy allow.

A much shorter (5½ miles round trip) but less scenic approach is via the Smith Brook trail (Hike 49), which joins the Pacific Crest Trail at Union Gap 1 mile from the road. The Crest Trail leads south from the Gap 1¾ miles to Lake Valhalla.

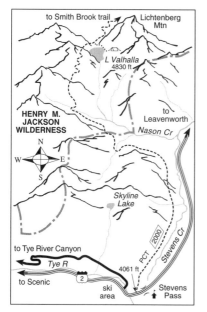

Cow parsnip

123

49 LAKE JANUS AND GRIZZLY PEAK

Round trip to Grizzly Peak
  17 miles
Hiking time 6–8 hours
High point 5597 feet
Elevation gain 1500 feet in,
  600 feet out
Hikable mid-July through October

One day or backpack
Map: Green Trails No. 144
  Benchmark
Current information: Ask at Lake
  Wenatchee Ranger Station
  about trail Nos. 1590 and 2000

A beautiful alpine lake and a long ridge trail, sometimes in Western Washington and sometimes in Eastern Washington and sometimes straddling the fence. An easy but spectacular stretch of the Pacific Crest Trail. The trip can be done in a day, but at least a weekend should be planned—the lake is inviting and so is "looking around the next corner."

Drive US 2 east 4 miles from Stevens Pass and turn left on Smith Brook road No. 6700. Cross Nason Creek bridge, turn left, and follow the road 3.5 miles toward Rainy Pass to the Smith Brook trailhead, elevation 3800 feet. (Parking is precarious on the narrow road here and is better done on the switchbacks below.)

Climb 1 mile on trail No. 1590 to 4680-foot Union Gap and the junction with the Pacific Crest Trail. Turn right, dropping 600 feet down the west side of the crest to round cliffs of Union Peak, then regaining part of the elevation before reaching 4146-foot Lake Janus, 2½ miles from the gap. The trail goes through pleasant forest in the far-off sound of Rapid River. Though the grade is gentle the tread is badly eroded in places.

The lake is everything an alpine lake should be—sparkling water surrounded by meadows and tall trees and topped by the bright green slopes of 6007-foot Jove Peak. Numerous camps are available, but finding one vacant is a rare chance on weekends. Those near the shore have been closed for rehabilitation. Forget wood fires; carry a stove.

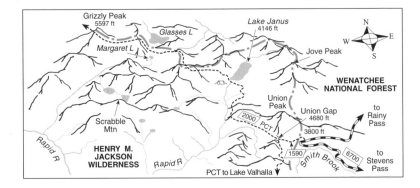

Lake Janus

From the lake the trail enters forest on smooth and easy tread, climbs 1100 feet in 1½ miles to the Cascade Crest (good camps here), contours around the Eastern Washington side of a small hill, and ducks around a corner back to Western Washington, a process repeated frequently on the way to Grizzly Peak. Carry water; there's little to be found here.

Every turn of the crest-wandering trail offers new views. Look east down into Lake Creek and Little Wenatchee River drainage and across to nearby Labyrinth Mountain. Look north to Glacier Peak. Look west down to the Rapid River and out to peaks above the Skykomish. At 2½ miles from Lake Janus is a glimpse of Margaret Lake, some 400 feet below the trail. A short ½ mile beyond is a view down to Glasses Lake and larger Heather Lake; this is a good turnaround point for day-hikers.

At about 5¼ miles from Lake Janus the trail climbs within a few feet of the top of 5597-foot Grizzly Peak and more panoramas. The trail also goes close to the summit of a nameless peak with a view of Glacier Peak; succumbing to this temptation will lead to further temptations on and on along the Pacific Crest Trail.

50 NASON RIDGE

One-way trip 16 miles
Allow 2–3 days
High point 6600 feet
Elevation gain 4200 feet
Hikable mid-July through
October

Map: Green Trails No. 145
Wenatchee Lake
Current information: Ask at Lake
Wenatchee Ranger Station
about trail No. 1583

The magnificent 26-mile journey the full length of Nason Ridge, through forest and wide-sky highlands from near the Pacific Crest Trail to near Lake Wenatchee, is a prime tour for experienced navigators. Unfortunately, the first 5 miles from Rainy Pass to Snowy Creek have never been built and the last 6½ miles to Lake Wenatchee are so muddled up by logging roads and harassed by motorcycles as to be no fun; the 16 miles between Snowy Creek and Round Mountain road, though, are superb.

The trip can best be done with two cars. Leave one at the Snowy Creek trailhead (Hike 51), elevation 3531 feet, and drive to the Round Mountain trailhead (Hike 54), elevation 3900.

Climb a steep 1000 feet in 1½ miles to the junction with Nason Ridge trail No. 1583 on Round Mountain and go left up a wooded ridge to within ¼ mile of 6237-foot Alpine Lookout (well worth the detour). From the lookout the trail drops to Merritt Lake (Hike 53) and campsites, 9 miles from the start.

Still in timber, the trail continues downward. In 1 mile keep right at a junction with the Merritt Lake trail. Ascend forest to a 5400-foot high point and drop to a crossing of Royal Creek and campsites at 4900 feet. Now the way climbs into meadowland, passing tiny Crescent Lake, 5500 feet, to a 6000-foot high point and skirting Rock Lake to a

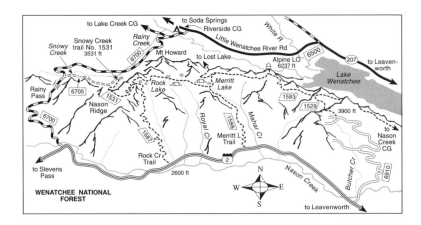

Rock Lake

junction with the Rock Mountain trail (Hike 52), 12 miles from the car. Camp in established sites in the trees near Crescent and Rock Lakes and not in the fragile meadows surrounding them.

Endless switchbacks take the trail to the 6400-foot shoulder of Rock Mountain, followed by a final drop to the Snowy Creek trailhead (Hike 51).

51 SNOWY CREEK–ROCK MOUNTAIN

Round trip 9 miles
Hiking time 6 hours
High point 6852 feet
Elevation gain 3350 feet
Hikable mid-July through
   October

One day or backpack
Map: Green Trails No. 145
   Wenatchee Lake
Current information: Ask at Lake
   Wenatchee Ranger Station
   about trail No. 1583

Forest, meadows, and switchbacks through the sky lead to the summit of Rock Mountain. This is a much more civilized route than the Rock Mountain trail (Hike 52). It starts 900 feet higher and has cool shade for hours after the other is so hot you can hear the ants sizzling.

Drive US 2 east 4 miles from Stevens Pass and turn left on Smith Brook road No. 6700 (Hike 49). Cross Rainy Pass and about 5 miles from the highway, at a major switchback, go straight ahead on road No. 6705 another 3.6 miles to a crossing of Snowy Creek and the trailhead, elevation 3531 feet.

Snowy Creek trail No. 1531 heads into magnificent old-growth forest. At 2 long miles, 4600 feet, is a fine campsite in upper Snowy Creek Basin, a large meadow flat enclosed by a horseshoe of cliffy peaks. Tread vanishes in the meadow, then reappears halfway across, on the left. The next 2 miles (steep and dry) enter trees, leave them for flower fields, and gain 2000 feet to the summit ridge of Rock Mountain. Here is a junction with the Nason Ridge–Rock Mountain trail. Go left on the crest to the lookout site atop Rock Mountain, 6852 feet, and the glorious views described in Hike 52.

Nason Ridge from Snowy Creek trail

Rock Mountain

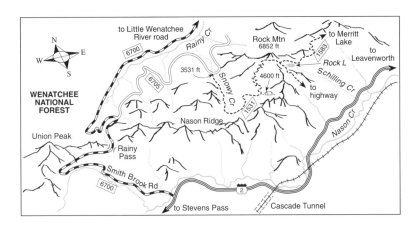

52   ROCK MOUNTAIN

Round trip 11 miles
Hiking time 8 hours
High point 6852 feet
Elevation gain 4250 feet
Hikable mid-July through
October

One day or backpack
Map: Green Trails No. 145
Wenatchee Lake
Current information: Ask at Lake
Wenatchee Ranger Station
about trail No. 1587

Broad meadows and a cold little lake enhance Rock Mountain, the scenic climax of Nason Ridge. However, the person who chooses this route to the top, rather than Snowy Creek (Hike 51), must be young and stubborn or old and ornery. The trail is very steep, despite 95 switchbacks. It lies on a south slope swept clean of shade trees by fire and avalanche. No water—unless you swallow a few thousand of the flies which, in season, fling themselves into your gasping mouth.

From the east, drive US 2 east 8.8 miles from Nason Creek Rest Area. From the west, cross Stevens Pass and drive 8.5 miles (0.4 mile past the Highway Department buildings). Near milepost 73 find a small parking area and the Rock Mountain trail sign, elevation 2600 feet.

Rock Mountain trail No. 1587 begins on a powerline service road. In about ⅓ mile go left, climbing steeply to the highest powerline pylon at about ⅔ mile, 3000 feet.

True trail commences, narrow and rocky, switchbacking up the naked bones of the mountain. Views, of course, begin immediately and never quit. The massive high bulk of the Chiwaukum Mountains, across the valley, dominates. A bit to the west, the green slopes of Arrowhead Mountain and Jim Hill Mountain grow greener the higher you climb. At about 3½ miles, 5000 feet, the wayside vegetation shifts to the subalpine—blueberries, heather, and shrubby Christmas trees (mighty thin shade). At 4½ miles, 6000 feet, is a junction with the Nason Ridge trail.

For Rock Lake turn right on the ridge trail, contouring several hundred feet above the lake. The snowfields that generally fill the basin

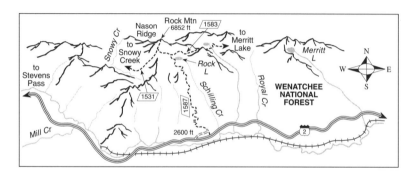

Rock Mountain trail

until late July may be mighty tempting to feet that have been frying for hours on the sunny side of the ridge. Don't camp in the fragile meadows by the lake inlet. Find nice sites in the trees just above and to the northeast of the shore.

For Rock Mountain turn left on the ridge trail, switchbacking, then following a spur ridge, and switchbacking again to the summit ridge and a junction with the Snowy Creek trail (Hike 51). Steep snow may force a party to detour or call it a day or call Mountain Rescue.

The summit ridge is an easy walk to the old lookout site atop Rock Mountain, 6852 feet, 5½ miles from the highway. The views extend north to Sloan Peak and Glacier Peak, south to the tip of Mt. Rainier rising above Mt. Daniel, and straight down 1000 feet to Rock Lake.

53   MERRITT LAKE

Round trip 6 miles
Hiking time 4 hours
High point 5003 feet
Elevation gain 2000 feet
Hikable late June through
   October

One day or backpack
Map: Green Trails No. 145
   Wenatchee Lake
Current information: Ask at Lake
   Wenatchee Ranger Station
   about trail No. 1588

Merritt Lake is a delightful tarn ringed by subalpine forest and enclosed by 6000-foot peaks. Fishermen, botanizers, and esthetes swarm. Nearby is another popular lake—the largest on Nason Ridge—that goes by the name of "Lost." Some hikers do indeed become lost, and wounded, too, because the trail is difficult and treacherous, definitely not for the inexperienced wayfarer.

Coming from the east, drive US 2 west 6 miles from Nason Creek Rest Area. From the west, drive east 11.4 miles from Stevens Pass to 3.3 miles beyond the Highway Department buildings. Near milepost 76 turn north on road No. 657 for 1.6 miles to the road-end and the start of Merritt Lake trail No. 1588, elevation 3000 feet.

The trail switchbacks up through a scattering of splendid old ponderosa pine and Douglas fir. At 2 miles skirt a boulder field and cross a small creek. At 2½ miles is a junction with Nason Ridge trail No. 1583 (Hike 50) and at 3 miles, Merritt Lake, 5003 feet. Numerous camps lie in the woods, handy to an open-air privy. Campers will want to carry a stove; the scene was picked clean of good burning wood by fishermen a couple of generations ago.

For Lost Lake, follow the Nason Ridge trail up and away from Merritt Lake a very scant ½ mile to a junction. The ridge trail ascends right to Alpine Lookout. Go left on the unmarked Lost Lake route, climbing to a 5500-foot pass and then descending, initially at an easy grade but soon in a steep and slippery draw, sharing the trail with a

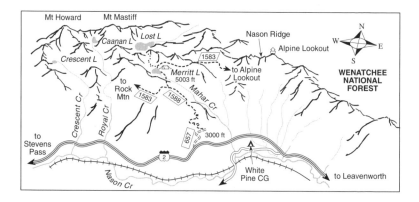

Merritt Lake

creek. People with slippery shoes and a tendency to break bones easily shouldn't try it. The route is straight down to the lake, 4930 feet. Aside from fish, there isn't much to see. Keep in mind the 650-foot climb on the return; add 3 miles and 3 hours to the round trip.

54 ALPINE LOOKOUT

Round trip 10 miles
Hiking time 5 hours
High point 6237 feet
Elevation gain 2400 feet
Hikable mid-June through
   September

One day
Map: Green Trails No. 145
   Wenatchee Lake
Current information: Ask at Lake
   Wenatchee Ranger Station
   about trail Nos. 1529 and 1583

Nason Ridge has a reputation as the very definition of "grueling." That, of course, is only accurate insofar as it refers to certain stretches of certain trails. This route, for example, hardly gets up enough sweat for a hiker to notice there is no water. Yet the views are broad, the flowers pretty. Moreover, chances are very good of spotting mountain goats in the small no-hunting area around Alpine Lookout. Further, as one of the last lookouts still active for fire detection, Alpine is a living vignette of history. The 1994 Round Mountain fire damaged part of this trail, but in a few years black will turn to the silver of bleached snags amid the rainbow of flower fields.

Alpine Lookout and mountain goat

Drive US 2 east 17 miles from Stevens Pass to Nason Creek Rest Area and 0.3 mile beyond. Pass a private driveway and turn left on Butcher Creek road No. 6910 (not signed). Cross Nason Creek, avoid spur roads to private homes, cross Nason Creek, enter National Forest land, and start climbing. At 4.5 miles from the highway go right on road No. 6910-170. At 4.7 miles reach Round Mountain trail No. 1529, elevation 3900 feet.

The first 1½ miles are typically "Nason," climbing steeply to meet Nason Ridge trail No. 1583, at 5300 feet. Go left. The next 3 miles are also less than perfect joy because the Forest Service currently gives motorcycles free run to the lookout junction. The trail (wheel road) contours the side of Round Mountain and gains almost 1000 feet to the junction. A short wheelfree spur leads to Alpine Lookout, 6237 feet, 5 miles from the road.

Mountain goat

The views are north to cliffs of Dirtyface Mountain, above waters of Lake Wenatchee, and south to the Stuart Range, Chiwaukum Mountains, and other peaks of the Alpine Lakes Wilderness.

The best times to see goats are early and late in the day. Don't wander about searching. Sit still, be quiet, and wait for them to come near you. Don't visit the lookout sanctuary during hunting season, when your presence might frighten the animals out of their small safe spot into the rifle sights.

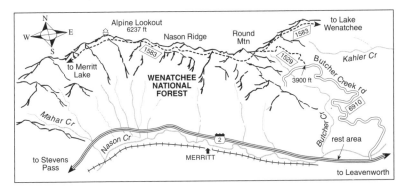

135

55   MINOTAUR LAKE

Round trip 6 miles
Hiking time 5 hours
High point 5550 feet
Elevation gain 2000 feet
Hikable mid-July through
   October

One day or backpack
Map: Green Trails No. 144
   Benchmark
Current information: Ask at Lake
   Wenatchee Ranger Station
   about trail No. 1517

Minotaur Lake lies in a Grecian setting. Above and beyond are the rock walls of 6376-foot Labyrinth Mountain. Below is Theseus Lake. Heather meadows and alpine firs complete the mythological scene. No longer are seven girls and seven boys annually given in sacrifice to Minotaur, but each year visitors pay (in season) a tribute to the gods as the bugs take a libation of blood. *Note:* The Forest Service lists this trail as a "route."

Drive US 2 east from Stevens Pass 19 miles and turn left to Lake Wenatchee. Pass the state park roads, at 1.8 miles beyond the Lake Wenatchee Ranger Station go left on Little Wenatchee River road No. 65 for another 6.2 miles, turn left again, cross the river on road No. 6700 for 6.2 miles, then go right on road No. 6704 (this junction also can be reached from the Smith Brook–Rainy Pass road No. 6700, Hike 51) and 1 more mile to the trailhead, elevation 3800 feet.

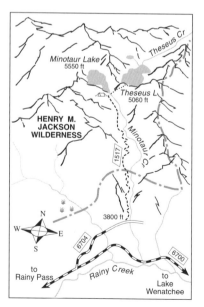

Minotaur Lake trail (route) No. 1517 is maintained but muddy. The way switchbacks up a hill, drops to cross an unnamed creek, and becomes a fishermen's path shooting straight up. There is no formal tread, only the groove pounded by many boots, gaining 1500 feet in the next mile. Views are limited to a few glimpses out through trees. At the end of the long, steep, dry ascent the trail turns downvalley ½ mile, losing 100 feet, then turns again and heads up Minotaur Creek. Forest gives way to highland meadows and at 3 miles is 5550-foot Mino-taur Lake.

In trees around the shore are several good campsites, a mob scene on weekends. Carry a stove; the last good firewood was burned up in 1937. Cross the outlet and walk a few yards northeast to see 5060-foot Theseus Lake; a very steep path leads down to more good camps (no fires here, either) and the shores of the lake.

For broader views of mountains west to Stevens Pass, north to Glacier Peak, and east beyond Lake Wenatchee, scramble easily to open ridges above the lakes and wander the crests.

Theseus Lake

56

HEATHER LAKE

Round trip 6½ miles
Hiking time 4 hours
High point 3953 feet
Elevation gain 1200 feet
Hikable July through October
One day or backpack

Map: Green Trails No. 144
  Benchmark
Current information: Ask at Lake
  Wenatchee Ranger Station
  about trail No. 1526

Waters of the ½-mile-long lake-in-the-woods reflect rocks and gardens of Grizzly Peak. A family could be happy here for days, prowling about from a comfortable basecamp. So could doughty adventurers seeking more strenuous explorations. The bad news is that on summer weekends it's often impossible to find a campsite.

From the upper end of Lake Wenatchee (Hike 55), drive 6 miles on Little Wenatchee River road No. 65, turn left on road No. 6700, cross the river, and in 0.6 mile go right on road No. 6701, following the river upstream. In 4.7 miles turn left onto road No. (6701)400. In 300 feet keep right and in another 2.3 miles reach the trailhead at the road-end, elevation 2800 feet.

The trail is a constant joy (nearly). The minor ups and downs of the first 1½ miles, netting only 100 feet, ease muscles into their task. Having done so, it turns stern, crossing Lake Creek on a bridge and heading up seriously, leaving no doubt why horses are forbidden. At 1½ miles is the boundary of the Henry M. Jackson Wilderness. In 2½ miles, after gaining 900 feet, the grade relents and joy resumes in the last ¾ mile to Heather Lake, 3953 feet, with fine camps and a cozy privy.

The bare schist near the lake outlet displays the grinding done by the glacier that scooped out the lake basin. Once these slabs were smooth, but eons of erosion have eaten away the polish, leaving only the grooves.

Attractive to the ambitious navigator with USGS map and compass, a way trail rounds the left side of the lake. At the far end follow a small

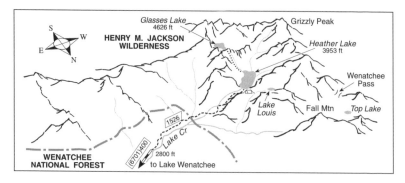

Heather Lake

stream south, climbing 700 feet in ½ mile to Glasses Lake, 4626 feet, so named because from neighboring peaks it looks like a pair of eyeglasses. No fires at either lake. There is also no heather at Heather Lake.

57 POET RIDGE–IRVING PASS

"The Bump"
Round trip 6 miles
Hiking time 4 hours
High point 6000 feet
Elevation gain 1900 feet

Poe Mountain
Round trip 7 miles
Hiking time 5 hours
High point 6015 feet
Elevation gain 2200 feet

Hikable mid-June to October
One day
Maps: Green Trails No. 144 Benchmark
Current information: Ask at Lake Wenatchee Ranger Station about
trail Nos. 1545 and 1543

Hike a difficult path, more a route than a trail, to a viewpoint bump on Poet Ridge in the Wenatchee Mountains, or, as many do, continue on to Poe Mountain. However, if Poe is the destination, most hikers find Hike 58 easier, though it starts at a lower elevation.

Drive Little Wenatchee River road No. 65 (Hike 58) for 9.6 miles (exactly 1 mile past Soda Springs Campground). Go right on road No. 6504. At 4.3 miles from the river road go right at an unmarked junction another 2 miles and find Irving Pass trail No. 1545 at a switchback, elevation 4200 feet.

The trail climbs a very steep 700 feet in what the sign says is ½ mile to Irving Pass, 4900 feet. Straight ahead from the junction here is the abandoned Panther Creek trail. Go left, climbing steeply a short ¼ mile to a second junction (unmarked). The right-hand trail contours down to Cockeye Creek and a pleasant camp.

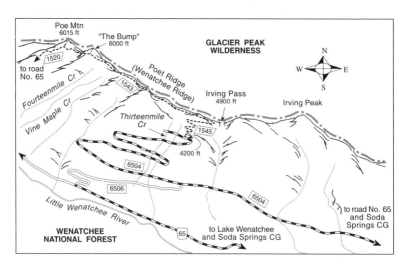

Keep to the crest an ever-deteriorating tread climbing over and around bumps atop Poet Ridge. Views begin to open up in another ½ mile as the trail crosses the top of steep meadows.

At approximately 3 miles from the road, the trail passes below the 6000-foot "The Bump" on Poet Ridge and starts down. Views now include the Wenatchee Range, Nason Ridge, Mt. Stuart, Mt. Rainier south, and peaks of Poet Ridge north. This is the time for a decision. What you will see atop 6015-foot Poe Mountain is practically the same as what you see here, so if the 15 extra feet are of no interest, call it a day and wander up the boot-beaten path to "The Bump."

If you must get Poe, from the high point follow the trail across a green bench, drop 100 feet to a timbered saddle, and contour around Poe Mountain, losing another 200 feet. Join trail No. 1520 (Hike 58) and climb to the 6015-foot top.

"The Bump" on Poet Ridge trail

58 POE MOUNTAIN

Round trip 6 miles
Hiking time 4 hours
High point 6015 feet
Elevation gain 3000 feet
Hikable late June through
October

One day
Map: Green Trails No. 144
Benchmark
Current information: Ask at Lake
Wenatchee Ranger Station
about trail No. 1520

What the map calls "Wenatchee Ridge" is unofficially known as "Poet Ridge," due to a government mapmaker of yore having named its various high points Bryant Peak, Longfellow Mountain, Poe Mountain, Irving Peak, and Whittier Peak. Discriminating students of literature call it "Poetaster Ridge" and lament the taste of government map-makers of yore. Poe is not the highest of the lot but has so commanding a view it was once the site of a lookout cabin. The panorama includes

Poet Ridge and Glacier Peak from Poe Mountain

the Little Wenatchee River valley from Meander Meadow to Soda Springs, forests of Nason Ridge, and mountains of the Cascade Crest. Views in other directions are blocked by various poets. Glacier Peak, Sloan, Monte Cristo, Hin-man, and Rainier can be seen above distant ridges.

The two trails to Poe Mountain are the same length. The better choice on a hot day would be the ridge route, reached from road No. 6504, starting at an elevation of 4200 feet (Hike 57). The direct route from the west described here should be done early in the morning before the sun blisters the trail. Carry water; there's none along the way save dewdrops.

Drive US 2 east from Stevens Pass 19 miles and turn left to Lake Wenatchee. Pass the state park road, cross the Wenatchee River bridge, stay left another 4.6 miles to the Lake Wenatchee Ranger Station. Go another 1.8

Columbine

mile to a Y, then left on No. 65, Little Wenatchee River road, 14.8 miles to its end, elevation 3000 feet. (Note that the last 2 miles are very primitive, winding around big old-growth trees.)

Walk ¼ mile on Little Wenatchee River trail No. 1525 and turn right on Poe Mountain trail No. 1520. The rate of gain is about 1000 feet per mile, ideal for getting there firstest with the mostest rubber left on the lugs. Shade trees are scarce but views are plentiful, enlarging at each upward rest-step. Just below the top the way joins the ridge trail, No. 1543, for the final ¼ mile to the meadowy summit.

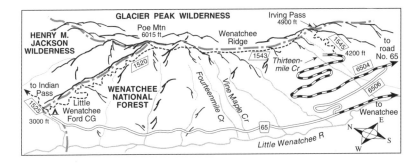

59 MEANDER MEADOW– KODAK PEAK

Round trip to Meander Meadow
12 miles
High point 5400 feet
Elevation gain 2400 feet
Round trip to Kodak Peak
16 miles
High point 6121 feet
Elevation gain 3100 feet

Hikable July to October
One day or backpack
Map: Green Trails No. 144
Benchmark
Current Information: Ask at Lake
Wenatchee Ranger Station
about trail No. 1525

Perhaps the easiest way in the Wenatchee area to sample the glories of the high country. A forest-and-meadow valley floor, a steep-and-hot struggle, and finally a superb little basin of grass and flowers and slow deep meanders of the headwaters stream. Above lie parklands of the Cascade Crest and endless easy wandering with views to everywhere.

From the Lake Wenatchee Ranger Station drive 1.8 miles, then go left 14.8 miles on Little Wenatchee River road No. 65 (Hike 58) to its end at the Little Wenatchee Ford Campground and trailhead, elevation 3000 feet, and find Little Wenatchee River trail No. 1525.

In ¼ mile pass the Poe Mountain trail junction. The first 4 miles are gently up and down, a net gain of only 700 feet, alternating between forest and glade and frequent stream crossings. The easy part ends at the edge of a vast meadow; here are a small creek and a campsite. The next 2 miles, gaining 1300 feet, may require courage and fortitude in the heat of the afternoon sun in fly season. The way climbs grass and brush, through sometimes-soggy greenery where at times the tread is hard to follow. Once above the meadow, in a mix of trees and avalanche paths, the tread is distinct but steep. Fortunately the views grow with every step. At 6 miles the trail drops a short bit into the basin of 5000-foot Meander Meadow; the camps are splendid and so are the hours of flower walking.

The trail crosses a meandering fragment of the Little Wenatchee

Meander Meadow

River and climbs another open mile and 500 more feet to a ridge and trail fork. Go either way—north or south of a small hill—to join the Pacific Crest Trail at 5400-foot Sauk Pass.

The junction with the Crest Trail gives the first view of Glacier Peak and marks the boundary of the Glacier Peak Wilderness. Walk north ½ mile to a 5630-foot saddle on the east ridge of Kodak Peak. Climb a boot-beaten path through blossoms another ½ mile to the 6121-foot summit and start cranking film through the Kodak. For more exploring see Hike 60.

The return trip can be made by going south 2 miles farther on the Crest Trail and then left on Cady Ridge trail No. 1532 some 5 miles to the starting point or by way of Cady Pass (Hike 60).

Sloan Peak from Pacific Crest Trail

LITTLE WENATCHEE RIVER
Henry M. Jackson Wilderness

60 CADY PASS–MEANDER MEADOW LOOP

**Loop trip 17½ miles, sidetrip
14 miles more
Allow 3–5 days
High point 4600 feet, sidetrip
6450 feet
Elevation gain 3000 feet, for sidetrip add 2400 feet**

**Hikable July through September
Map: Green Trails No. 144
Benchmark
Current information: Ask at Lake
Wenatchee Ranger Station
about trail Nos. 1501, 1525, and
2000**

A loop hike splendid in its own right, and a sidetrip, if desired, to White Pass along what some argue is the most beautiful segment of the entire Pacific Crest National Scenic Trail, certainly one of the longest meadow walks anywhere in the Cascade Range.

Drive the east side of Lake Wenatchee and 1.8 miles beyond the Lake Wenatchee Ranger Station go left 14.8 miles on Little Wenatchee River road No. 65 (Hike 58) to its end near Little Wenatchee Ford Campground, elevation 3000 feet.

Trail No. 1501 drops to a bridge over the Little Wenatchee River. In ¼ mile pass the Cady Ridge trail and at 3½ miles a nice camp beside Cady Creek. Follow the creek 5 miles, gaining 1700 feet (including ups and downs), to wooded and waterless 4300-foot Cady Pass. Turn right (north) on the Pacific Crest Trail, climbing 1300 feet in 2 miles to break out above timberline on the divide between Cady Creek and Pass Creek. Now the way goes around this side or that of one small knoll after another, alternating between Eastern Washington and Western Washington. Then comes a traverse along the east slope of 6368-foot Skykomish Peak. At 2½ miles from Cady Pass (8 miles from the road) is 5479-foot Lake Sally Ann, a charming little tarn amid cliff-bordered meadows, very fragile and in the past badly abused. Camping with stock is now banned, as are fires within 200 feet of the lake. Less than ½ mile farther is an intersection with the Cady Ridge trail and another camp in a broad meadow. Climb a waterfall-sparkling basin to 5680-foot Wards Pass and roam parkland atop and near the crest past Dishpan Gap to 5450-foot Sauk Pass, 5½ miles from Cady Pass (10½ miles from the road), and a junction with trail No. 1525, the return route by way of Meander Meadow (Hike 60). For a basecamp descend meadows to the campsites or proceed on the crest a mile farther to superlative spots.

For the sidetrip continue on the Crest Trail 7 miles to 6450-foot Red Pass, more flower-covered meadows, and a spectacular view of Glacier Peak. The way goes up (1900 feet) and down (900 feet) the ridge top, totalling for the round trip 14 miles of hiking and 2400 feet of climbing—worth it.

The sidetrip begins by traversing green slopes of Kodak Peak to a saddle. (Take a few minutes to carry your camera to the 6121-foot summit.) Descend across a gorgeous alpine basin and down forest to mostly wooded Indian Pass, 5000 feet, 1½ miles from Sauk Pass. Find pleasant campsites in the pass—but usually no water except in early summer.

Climb forest and gardens around the side of Indian Head Peak to tiny Kid Pond and beyond to 5378-foot Lower White Pass, 3 miles from Sauk Pass, and a junction with the White River trail. The next 1½ miles have the climax meadows, past Reflection Pond into flower fields culminating at 5904-foot White Pass, 4½ miles from Sauk Pass. For dramatic views of Glacier Peak and the White Chuck Glacier walk the Crest Trail west another 1½ miles to Red Pass.

Having done (or not) the sidetrip, finish the loop from Meander Meadow by following trail No. 1525 down 2 miles of flowers and another 4 miles of forest and meadow.

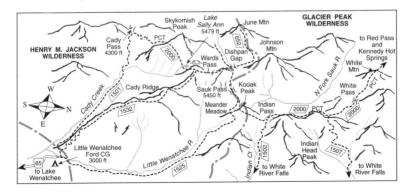

61 DIRTYFACE PEAK

Round trip 9½ miles
Hiking time 7 hours
High point 5984 feet
Elevation gain 4000 feet
Hikable mid-June through
October

One day
Map: Green Trails No. 145
Wenatchee Lake
Current information: Ask at Lake
Wenatchee Ranger Station
about trail No. 1500

A stiff climb, cruelly hot in sunny and windless weather, to a deserted lookout site with an airy view over Lake Wenatchee and into the Glacier Peak Wilderness. The last 2½ miles are dry; carry lots of water. For hikers who don't mind a few small snowpatches, this is a fine mid-June trip.

Drive US 2 east from Stevens Pass 19 miles and turn left to Lake Wenatchee. Pass the state park road, cross the Wenatchee River bridge, and stay left another 4.6 miles to the Lake Wenatchee Ranger Station. Turn right, behind the station, to find the trailhead, elevation 2000 feet.

The trail is mostly in very good shape, wide and smooth, but steep, very steep, gaining about 1000 feet a mile. (The trail sign says the peak is 4 miles but the distance is definitely 4½ miles or more.) In the first mile are several creeks. At 1½ miles intersect an abandoned logging road, follow it a scant ½ mile to its end, and pick up the trail again. Here is a good campsite in the woods, and also the last water.

Phlox

The way relentlessly climbs 70 switchbacks (we counted them) to the summit ridge. At about switchback 45 the trail leaves the tall ponderosa pine and enters alpine trees and flowers—and glorious views of the lake. From the crest it is almost ½ mile and 11 more switchbacks (for a total of 81) to the old lookout site at 5984 feet.

Enjoy views west to Nason Ridge, north up the Napeequa River to Clark Mountain, Chiwawa Ridge, and the Chiwawa valley, and east to endless hills. Below to the left is Fish Lake and, directly beneath, Lake Wenatchee. At the head of the latter, note the vast marshes and the meandering streams; at one point the White River comes within a few feet of

Lake Wenatchee from Dirtyface Lookout site

the lake but snakes back another ¼ mile before entering. Ant-sized boats can be seen on the lakes, and cars on the highways.

In early July the rock gardens are snowfield-brilliant in blossoming phlox. In late summer and fall the upper trail offers blueberries to sate a perhaps gigantic thirst.

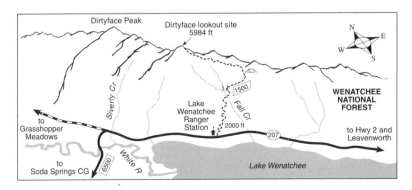

62 TWIN LAKES

Round trip 8 miles
Hiking time 5 hours
High point 2825 feet
Elevation gain 1000 feet
Hikable June through October

Map: Green Trails No. 145
    Wenatchee Lake
Current information: Ask at Lake
    Wenatchee Ranger Station
    about trail No. 1503

A forest walk past magnificent cedar trees to two large, shallow lakes. The trail is so rough and, in places, so very steep, that horses are banned.

Drive Highway 167 on the north side of Lake Wenatchee past the ranger station and go right on White River Road No. 6400 for 6.2 miles. Opposite the Napeequa Crossing Campground, find Twin Lakes trail No. 1503, elevation 2000 feet.

A few feet from the road the trail tips steeply upward, gaining 250 feet up a cliff in a long ¼ mile. A short sidetrip leads to a dramatic viewpoint down on the Tall Timber Ranch and Presbyterian Church Camp and upvalley to 7431-foot Mt. David. The trail then contours a hillside, enters Glacier Peak Wilderness in ¾ mile, and in dropping to near the Napeequa River, 1 mile from the road, loses all but 30 feet of the 250 feet.

The way levels, passes a swamp (maybe a beaver pond), and then climbs steadily up Twin Lakes Creek. About 2¾ miles a narrow gorge requires a short bit of hands-and-feet rock-scrambling. At 3¼ miles is the first and smallest of the Twin Lakes, 2822 feet.

Brush fences off the water. For views follow the trail around the north shore to bare rock or a bit farther to where beavers have gnawed down a large tree. In a scant 4 miles are a cabin built in 1949 by the State Game Department and a view of the 2-mile-long second Twin Lake, 2825 feet. Again the water is beyond reach.

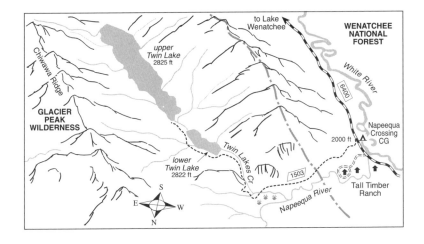

Lower Twin Lake

Mount Jonathan from Mount David trail

WHITE RIVER
Glacier Peak Wilderness

63   MOUNT DAVID

Round trip 16 miles
Hiking time 10 hours
High point 7431 feet
Elevation gain 5400 feet
Hikable mid-August to October
One day or backpack

Map: Green Trails No. 145
      Wenatchee Lake
Current information: Ask at
      Lake Wenatchee Ranger
      Station about trail No. 1521

   Climb a real mountain, 7431 feet high. However, though the ascent is lengthy and strenuous, the cliffy summit, where climbers would otherwise rope up, has a trail blasted to a long-abandoned lookout site.

(The cabin is gone, but the stone privy remains.) Enjoy panoramic views out over countless peaks and down almost a vertical mile to the river. It's best not to try the hike until August, when snow has melted from the steep and potentially dangerous gullies. The trail is dry, so carry plenty of water.

Drive from US 2 to Lake Wenatchee (Hike 61). Cross the Wenatchee River. At a big Y go left past the Ranger Station and at 6.4 miles from the bridge stay right on White River road No. 6400. At 16.5 miles from the bridge reach the road-end and parking area, elevation 2300 feet.

Cross the White River on a horse bridge signed "Indian Creek Trail." On the far side enter the Glacier Peak Wilderness and turn downstream on a trail signed "Mt. David" and "Panther Creek." In 1 long mile from the bridge, where the river trail keeps left, turn right on the Mt. David trail.

There is a big bundle of elevation to gain and the trail gets at it immediately. At ⅓ mile cross the last reliable stream. In 1 mile the tread is difficult to find in slide alder and vine maple of an avalanche slope. From here the trail is well graded. Relentless switchbacks grind up and up through forest to the ridge crest at 4½ miles.

The final 3½ miles follow ups and downs of the ridge, sometimes contouring below high points, switchbacking up one gully then moving to the next. Around several cliffs the trail has been eroded away, but is still safe. Views grow: south to Lake Wenatchee, Mt. Daniel, and Mt. Rainier and north to Clark Mountain.

Snow remains on slopes directly under the summit rocks until late August—a good reason for doing the trip no earlier. Tread is very obscure in a talus here and easily may be lost. If so, climb to the ridge and find the way where it crosses to the south side of the peak. The last few hundred feet have been blasted from cliff and improved by cement steps. Once there was even a guardrail, but it's gone now. Hikers suffering from acrophobia will be happier to settle for a conclusion somewhat short of the absolute top, 8 miles from the road.

Views are long to all horizons. Glacier Peak, 12 miles away, dominates, but careful study reveals many other mountains of the Cascade Crest; off west, above the head of Indian Creek, is Sloan Peak. Look down and down to the Indian Creek trail, crossing streamside meadows.

The only possible campsite is a flat meadow at about 5200 feet. The meadow is some 500 feet below the trail, reached by a spur descending from a short bit past the 4-mile marker.

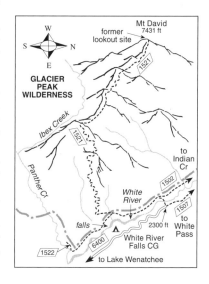

64 INDIAN CREEK– WHITE RIVER LOOP

Round trip to Indian Creek
8 miles
Hiking time 4 hours
High point 3200 feet
Elevation gain 900 feet
Hikable mid-June to October
One day or backpack

Loop trip to Indian Creek and
White River 28 miles
Allow 3–4 days
High point 5500 feet
Elevation gain 2200 feet
Hikable July to October

Maps: Green Trails No. 144 Benchmark, No. 145 Wenatchee Lake, No.
111 Sloan Peak, and No. 112 Glacier Peak
Current information: Ask at Lake Wenatchee Ranger Station about
trail Nos. 1502, 2000, and 1507 (ask about stream crossings on trail
No. 1507)

Study the recipes and choose your repast: a day hike in the deep woods; an easy or lengthier overnighter; or a loop trip of 3–5 days, tacking on a sidetrip through glory gardens of the Pacific Crest Trail.

Drive the White River road to the end (Hike 63), elevation 2300 feet.

The loop, equally good in either direction, is here described clockwise. Cross the river on the horse bridge and turn upstream on Indian Creek trail No. 1502, following the White River a long 2 miles. The way then crosses Indian Creek on a bridge and tilts, gaining 800 feet in 1¾ miles. Trail and creek abruptly level off at a nice campsite, 3200 feet, 4 miles from the road. This is a dandy turnaround for a day hike or a

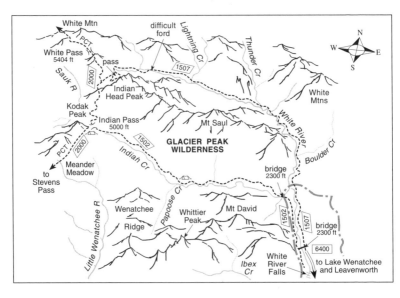

Indian Creek

short overnighter, though there are several other good camps the next 3 miles.

The 2 miles from the 3200-foot camp go up and down a lot, from solid ground to horse-churned mudholes, but make a net elevation gain of zero. The next 5 miles compensate by climbing moderately but steadily to Indian Pass, 5000 feet, 11 miles from the road. The camps here usually have no potable water after early summer.

Climb from parkland forest of the pass to flowers of the 5500-foot high point on the side of Indian Head Peak. Drop a bit to Lower White Pass, 5378 feet, and meet the White River trail at a scant 1½ miles from Indian Pass.

It would be a shame, having walked this far, not to romp through the gardens a little. Indeed, if you can't allow an extra day or two to sidetrip north on the Pacific Crest Trail—1 mile or 2, or the 4½ miles to Red Pass—why bother doing the loop?

The return leg descends from Lower White Pass on White River trail No. 1507. Some 4 miles from the pass a bridge over the river has been washed out. The footlogs (belly logs?) are slick. The alternative is to ford, which can be hazardous in high water, which lasts until mid-August. Consider the advantages of hiking counterclockwise, in order to confront the raging torrent on the way in, when you can readily turn back. Farther along are several long stretches of the sort of brush that thrives where avalanches forbid forests to do so. One stretch is 2 miles long. If you think you don't like it when the bushes are soaked with rain, wait until you've tried it in a blazing sun when the flies are so hungry they're eating the mosquitoes. Except for *that,* the way lies in cathedral stands of ancient-growth forest.

At 15 miles from Lower White Pass the loop returns to the road, for a total of 28 miles plus the side-romp north on the Cascade Crest.

65 NAPEEQUA VALLEY VIA BOULDER PASS

Round trip to Napeequa ford
26 miles
Allow 3–7 days
High point 6250 feet
Elevation gain 4000 feet in,
2000 feet out
Hikable August through
September

Maps: Green Trails No. 145
Wenatchee Lake and No. 113
Holden
Current information: Ask at Lake
Wenatchee Ranger Station
about trail Nos. 1507 and 1562

The Napeequa River has craftily designed its fabled "Shangri La" to keep people out—exiting from the valley via a cliff-walled gorge that has never had any sort of trail, entering from glaciers and precipices inaccessible except to climbers. Each of the only two reasonable hiker accesses is over an exceedingly high pass and a wide, deep, swift river. Hikers may well climb to the top of Boulder Pass, drop to the floor of Napeequa valley—and find themselves cut off from the meadows by the Napeequa River. Then, if they get across the flood alive, they can expect to be sucked dry of blood by flies as big as the flowers and as numerous. Pretty pictures don't tell the whole story.

Drive to the end of the White River road (Hike 63), elevation 2300 feet.

Hike White River trail No. 1507 a pleasant, virtually level 4 miles through lovely virgin forest to Boulder Pass trail No. 1562. Subsequent mileages are from this junction, 2550 feet.

The well-graded trail climbs steadily. In about 2½ miles is a crossing of Boulder Creek, hazardous in high water. At 4 miles is 5000-foot Basin Camp, under the walls of 8676-foot Clark Mountain. This is a logical and splendid spot to end the first day—and also a grand base for an extra day exploring a very faint path west to a 6150-foot saddle overlooking the White River. To find the path, cross the creek from camp to a point just under a slab of red rock on the opposite side of the valley. Even without tread the going would be fairly easy up open meadows.

From Basin Camp the trail climbs 2½ miles to 6250-foot Boulder

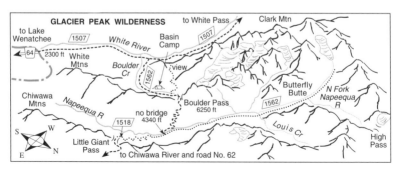

Pass, the meadowy saddle to the immediate east of Clark Mountain. Look down into the Napeequa valley and over to Little Giant Pass (Hike 70). The hike to here, 10¾ miles from the road, makes a strenuous but richly rewarding 2–3-day trip. You may well decide to say the heck with Shangri La and drowning.

Switchback down some 2000 feet in 2¼ miles to the valley floor—and trouble—at 4340 feet. The Forest Service is unable to keep a bridge across the swift-flowing Napeequa River, which perhaps can be safely forded at this point in late August. But many summers it's never less than very risky.

If you can manage to cross, explorations are limited only by the time available. Follow the trail up the wide, green valley floor, probably the floor of a Pleistocene lake, 5 or 6 miles; good camps are numerous. In ½ mile look to glaciers on Clark Mountain. In 2 miles pass under the falls of Louis Creek. Wander on and on, higher and higher, better and better, to trail's end in the moraines and creeks of Napeequa Basin, a deep hole half-ringed by dazzling glaciers, one of which tumbles nearly to the basin floor.

Napeequa River from ford

66 BASALT RIDGE–GARLAND PEAK

Round trip 9 miles
High point 6351 feet
Elevation gain 2500 feet
Hikable July to October
One day or backpack

Maps: Green Trails No. 145
    Wenatchee Lake, No. 146 Plain,
    and No. 114 Lucerne
Current information: Ask at Lake
    Wenatchee Ranger Station
    about trail Nos. 1530 and 1515

The trail along Basalt Ridge to the Garland Peak area of the Entiat
Mountains gives views across Rock Creek to Old Gib Mountain and be-
yond to the ice-gleaming spires of Clark Mountain and Glacier Peak.
There are four ways to reach Basalt Ridge: the hard way, Minnow
Creek; over the top of Basalt Peak; 5 miles up Rock Creek (Hike 68);
and the terribly steep (but short, only 1½ miles) access described here.

Drive US 2 between Stevens Pass and Leavenworth and turn north
on the Lake Wenatchee road. Cross the Wenatchee River bridge and go
straight ahead on Chiwawa Loop Road 1.4 miles, then left on the
Chiwawa River road 9.4 miles, then right on road No. 6210 for another
5.8 miles to trail No. 1530, elevation 3900 feet (don't mistake this for
trail No. 1539, at approximately 4 miles).

The trail starts steep, relents briefly, and reverts to type, henceforth
showing little mercy. In 1¼ miles the trail climbs 1200 feet to a 5200-
foot saddle and an unsigned junction with Basalt Ridge trail No. 1515.
Several hundred feet uphill to the left is the signed junction with the
access trail from Rock Creek. Go right along the saddle, losing about
50 feet, then climbing a moderately steep, rocky slope, emerging from
trees to buckbrush meadows. These give way to meadows that are almost all stones, very few plants.

At about 3 miles from the road the way attains a high point, 6351
feet, with views big enough to satisfy the day-hiker—who by now will
have been laboring 2 or 3 or 4 hours. Overnighters will continue, losing

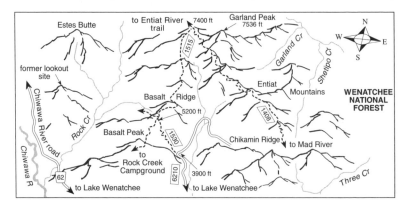

Basalt Ridge trail

about 200 feet, gaining them back, and contouring the slopes of a knob to a 6500-foot saddle at the edge of a huge pumice field (deposited by Glacier Peak 12,000 years ago). Descend a way trail 500 feet to campsites—and the only water of the trip—below Garland Peak.

For explorations, continue on the Basalt Ridge trail to the Garland Peak trail (Hike 86) and proceed north or south.

67 SCHAEFER LAKE

Round trip 10 miles
Hiking time 6 hours
High point 5131 feet
Elevation gain 2700 feet
Hikable July (if a safe crossing
**   can be found) through October**

One day or backpack
Map: Green Trails No. 145
**   Wenatchee Lake**
Current information: Ask at Lake
**   Wenatchee Ranger Station**
**   about trail No. 1519**

A forest trail leads to a sparkling lake amid rocky ridges. First, however, a person must get to the trail, which lies on the far side of the Chiwawa River, only safe to wade in late summer. So, is the good old logjam still in place? It moves every winter. Thereby hangs the decision, to go or not to go.

Schaefer Lake

Drive the Chiwawa River road (Hike 66) 13.4 miles from Chiwawa Loop Road (county road No. 22) to upstream 0.2 mile from the Rock Creek Information Center and campground to Schaefer Creek trail No. 1519, elevation 2474 feet.

The trail drops to the river and—one hopes—the logjam is still there and safe to cross. On the far side the way pokes along the Chiwawa valley floor a magnificent mile of spruce and cedar forest. It then hits the valley wall and begins a long uphill traverse in the woods, with a couple of short switchbacks and occasional glimpses to snowy summits of Red Mountain, Dumbell, and Seven-Fingered Jack. At about 2½ miles a corner is rounded into the valley of Schaefer Creek, passing a possible camp just short of 3 miles and at 3½ miles crossing the creek on a sturdy bridge, 4100 feet.

Bear tracks

The trail now does business, climbing 1000 feet in 1¼ miles (at 4½ miles is the boundary of Glacier Peak Wilderness). The ascent slackens, passing Lower Schaefer Lake, a shallow pond, and reaching Upper Schaefer Lake at 5 miles, 5131 feet.

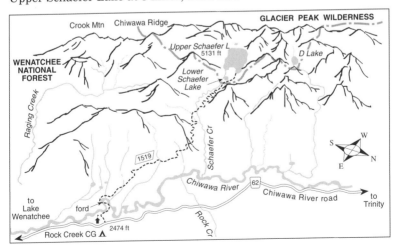

68   ROCK CREEK

Round trip 14 miles
Allow 2 days
High point 4300 feet
Elevation gain 1800 feet
Hikable mid-June to October

Maps: Green Trails No. 113 Holden
and No. 145 Wenatchee Lake
Current information: Ask at Lake
Wenatchee Ranger Station
about trail No. 1509

Looking for a spot just like Spider Meadow (Hike 74), except with the flowers outnumbering the hikers? This forest trail leads to campsites at the edge of Rock Creek Meadow, not as big as the Spider but equally beautiful. Unfortunately, the first 2 miles are open to motorcycles.

Drive the Chiwawa River road (Hike 66) 14.8 miles from Chiwawa Loop Road (county road No. 22). Just before the Rock Creek bridge find Rock Creek trail No. 1509 on the right side of the road, elevation 2515 feet.

Built wide and hard for heavy horse use, the trail climbs gently the first mile, steepens a bit the second mile, and at 2¼ miles, 3400 feet, comes to a junction. The right fork climbs to the Basalt Ridge trail (Hike 66); keep straight ahead, left. The trail, at this point some 400–500 feet above Rock Creek, contours (with ups and downs) the next 1¾ miles, letting the river catch up to the trail level.

At 4½ miles the route enters the Glacier Peak Wilderness, drops a bit, and enters a magnificent forest of big trees. Just beyond the 5-mile marker is a choice little campsite near the stream.

Starting at about 5½ miles, the trail is no more Mr. Nice Guy, becoming rough and steep. Occasional windows open in the forest to Devil's Smoke Stack, Fifth of July Mountain, and nameless peaks of the Entiat Mountains. At 6¼ miles is a crossing—difficult until late

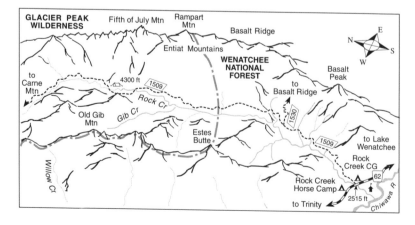

Rock Creek trail

summer—of Rock Creek. At 7 miles the way passes through the promised meadow to excellent campsites at the second crossing of the creek, 4300 feet.

For easy explorations from a basecamp here, continue upstream to more meadows or hike 5 more miles (gaining 2700 feet) to the lookout site on Carne Mountain (Hike 73). Consider a loop trip via Carne Mountain and Estes Butte (Hike 69); in addition to the above, add 10 miles, for a loop total of 22 miles, elevation gain of about 5000 feet.

Estes Butte

69   ESTES BUTTE

Round trip 6 miles
Hiking time 4 hours
High point 5397 feet
Elevation gain 2900 feet
Hikable June to October
One day

Maps: Green Trails No. 145
  Wenatchee Lake and No. 113
  Holden
Current information: Ask at Lake
  Wenatchee Ranger Station
  about trail No. 1527

A climb to a former lookout site on a 5402-foot bump on the ridge leading to Estes Butte. Do the hike in midsummer when the forest floor is blooming with sidebells pyrola and pipsissewa or on a crisp fall day when the sun cheers but doesn't overheat. The trail was rebuilt in 1995 to bear up under heavy horse traffic.

Drive the Chiwawa River road (Hike 66) 15 miles from Chiwawa Loop Road (county road No. 22). Find Estes Butte trail No. 1527 between Rock Creek bridge and the Rock Creek Horse Camp, elevation 2515 feet.

The trail parallels Rock Creek on the level along a rough old mining road. Long switchbacks then climb to the right at a grade ideal for horses; the slow pace gives plenty of time to look down to the pyrola and pipsissewa. The first mile has a few lookouts through chinks in the green wall to views down the valley, and in the second mile some windows open on green meadows of the Entiat Mountains to the east.

At 3 miles is the old lookout site. Cemented to a rock, a USGS marker says "5402 feet." The USGS map shows 5397. The building was atop a tower with an all-points view over the tree tops. Only the concrete foundation remains, but by moving about and looking between trees the same view can be assembled from the pieces. Day-trippers should eat their cookies here and go home.

The trail continues another 12 miles, with major ups and downs, over the tippy-top of 5942-foot Estes Butte, into the Glacier Peak Wilderness, around the side of Old Gib Mountain, to Carne Mountain (Hike 73), gaining 2500 feet on the way. The route is dangerous before the snow melts and bone-dry afterward.

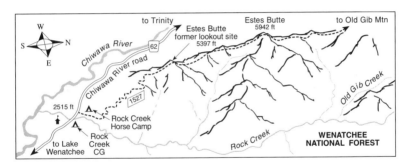

70 LITTLE GIANT PASS

Round trip to the pass 9½ miles
Hiking time 9 hours
High point 6409 feet
Elevation gain 4200 feet in, 300 feet out
Hikable early August through September

One day or backpack
  Holden
Map: Green Trails No. 113
Current information: Ask at Lake Wenatchee Ranger Station about trail No. 1518

Climb to the famous view of the fabled Napeequa valley. Look down on the silvery river meandering through green meadows of the old lakebed. See the gleaming ice on Clark Mountain and Tenpeak, glimpse a piece of Glacier Peak. But you gotta really want it. Strong mountaineers turn pale at memories of Little Giant in sunshine and flytime. However, this route to Napeequa valley, though more grueling than the Boulder Pass entry (Hike 65), is 5 miles shorter and has no fearsome ford of the Napeequa to face. Ah, but it may have a fearsome ford of the Chiwawa River. But that's at the very beginning, so you get the bad news in time to choose another destination should the logjam be missing and the flood be boiling halfway up your Kelty.

Drive the Chiwawa River road about 19 miles from Chiwawa Loop Road (county road No. 22) to Little Giant Pass trailhead No. 1518, elevation 2600 feet.

Longingly inspect remains of the bridge taken out by a flood in 1972. Look around for a logjam—they change every year. Finding nothing, try the wade, if you are fairly sure you can survive it, and if you do, follow abandoned roads through abandoned Maple Creek Campground toward the mountainside, and pretty soon pick up the trail. The old straight-up sheep driveway of evil reputation has been partly replaced (and the sheep are long gone from here, too) by a trail that was nicely engineered, if steep, but is deteriorating rapidly from lack of maintenance. The way climbs the valley of Maple Creek in pretty pine forest, crosses a saddle, and drops to South Fork Little Giant Creek at about 2½ miles from the river, 4000 feet. Campsites on both sides.

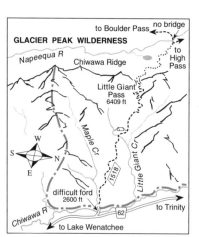

Now the way steepens and at 3 miles half-scrambles up a broad rib of bare schist that splits the valley in two and on a sunny day

Napeequa Valley from Little Giant Pass

will fry your boots. But in ⅓ mile creeks begin. So do camps that get progressively better, the last on a scenic meadow knoll at 4 miles. A lovely ascent in greenery and marmots leads to the 6409-foot pass, 4⅔ miles from the river.

Better views can be obtained by scrambling up the knobs on either side of the pass, which in addition to being a sensational grandstand is a glory of flowers.

The trail down to the Napeequa has been abandoned for years, yet suffices for hikers—but not for horses or sheep, and bleached bones prove it. Watch your step—at spots a misstep could add you to the casualty list. The distance to the 4200-foot valley floor is 2 miles, and if the views don't have you raving, the blossoms will. Or, in season, the flies. The abandoned trail proceeds upvalley 1⅓ miles to the site of the bridge that is gone and the ford that remains to cross the river to the Boulder Pass trail (Hike 65). The best camps hereabouts are on gravel bars—but watch out for sudden high water on hot afternoons.

71 BUCK CREEK PASS–HIGH PASS

Round trip 19 miles
Allow 2–3 days
High point 6000 feet
Elevation gain 3200 feet
Hikable July through October

Map: Green Trails No. 113 Holden
Current information: Ask at Lake
  Wenatchee Ranger Station
  about trail Nos. 1550, 1511, and
  1562

In a mountain range full to overflowing with "unique places," two things have given Buck Creek Pass fame: an unusual richness of flower gardens rising from creek bottoms to high summits, and the exceptional view of the grandest ice streams of Glacier Peak, seen across the broad, forested valley of the Suiattle River. The trail lends itself to a variety of trips short and long: a day's walk as far as time allows, a weekend at the pass, or a week of explorations.

Drive the Chiwawa River road (Hike 66) some 23 miles from Chiwawa Loop Road (county road No. 22) to the end at Phelps Creek, elevation 2772 feet.

Galcier Peak from Buck Creek Pass

Walk the trail bridge over Phelps Creek, skirt the private property in the old mining (wannabe but never really was) town of Trinity, and climb moderately along an abandoned road. At ¾ mile enter Glacier Peak Wilderness. In 1½ miles, at a Y where the road proceeds straight ahead toward mining claims on Red Mountain (Hike 72), the trail turns off left, going up and down within sound of the Chiwawa River. At 2¾ miles cross the "river" (here just a swift creek), then a low rib, into Buck Creek drainage. Just beyond the bridge is a large campsite.

The trail climbs a valley step, levels out and passes a forest camp in a patch of grass, switchbacks up another glacier-gouged step, and emerges from trees to traverse a wide avalanche meadow at 5 miles, 4300 feet. This is a good turnaround for a day hike, offering a view of the cliffs and hanging glaciers on the north wall of 8528-foot Buck Mountain.

Here begins a series of long switchbacks, climbing on a 10 percent grade to a 6000-foot high point overlooking Buck Creek Pass, 9½ miles. For camping, drop about 200 feet into the pass; the area is mobbed on weekends.

Explorations? Enough for a magnificent week.

Start with an evening wander to Flower Dome to watch Suiattle forests darken into night while the snows of Glacier Peak glow pink.

For a spectacular sunrise, carry your sleeping bag to the top of Liberty Cap.

Try an interesting sheepherders' track. Walk the main trail back toward Trinity about ½ mile from the pass to a large basin with several streams. A few feet before emerging from forest into basin meadows, go left on an unmarked way trail that traverses flower gardens below Helmet Butte and Fortress Mountain, passes delightful campsites, and disappears in some 2 miles at 6100 feet.

Don't miss the dead-end trail toward (not to) High Pass. Find it on the south side of Buck Creek Pass and ascend around Liberty Cap and as far as the way is not covered with dangerously steep snow. The end, 3 miles from Buck Creek Pass, is in a 7000-foot saddle overlooking the wintry basin of Triad Lake. Getting from trail's end to High Pass is for climbers only.

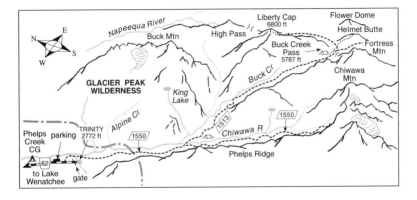

169

72 RED MOUNTAIN

Round trip 16½ miles
Allow 2 days
High point 6900 feet
Elevation gain 4100 feet
**Hikable mid-July through
    September**
**Map: Green Trails No. 113
    Holden**
**Current information: Ask at Lake
    Wenatchee Ranger Station
    about trail No. 1550**

Mining operations, mainly in the 1920s and 30s but with some messing around in the 1950s, have bruised and ripped and battered the fragile subalpine terrain. The old trail has been replaced by an ugly, rutted prospectors' road. Not for centuries will nature repair the damage. Keep it in mind as an object lesson next time you hear defenders of the antique mining laws bray about "free enterprise." Not all is lost, however. The surviving meadows are beautiful, and the views of the Upper Chiwawa River basin are splendid.

Drive the Chiwawa River road (Hike 66) some 23 miles to the end at Trinity–Phelps Creek, elevation 2772 feet.

Walk across the Phelps Creek trail bridge skirting Trinity "town" and follow trail signs to the Glacier Peak Wilderness at ¾ mile, and a Y at 1½ miles where Buck Creek Pass trail No. 1513 (Hike 71) branches left. Continue on the road—officially, Chiwawa River trail No. 1550— as it steadily ascends the valley on the flanks of Phelps Ridge, the way muddy from tromping by many hooves.

At 5¾ miles, 4750 feet, the route splits. The left fork is Chiwawa Basin trail No. 1550A, which is brushed out 1 mile farther into the basin, offering several appealing campsites. In days past the prospectors had a loop through the basin that rejoined the other fork high on Red Mountain.

Trail No. 1550, the right fork, sticks with the road, climbing through avalanche brush, then timber, in a series of long switchbacks. At the top of the last one is a fine campsite (if not recently used by horses) at the edge of a large green basin below the brightly colored rock slopes of Red Mountain.

The road-trail now cuts a broad scar across the meadows of Red Mountain, traversing toward the lower slopes of Chiwawa Mountain.

Camping on Red Mountain (photo by Kirkendall/Spring)

The end is on a talus where trails branch every which way to little holes in the ground. For excellent alpine camping, descend the rubble to open benches amid the all-around splashes of waterfalls.

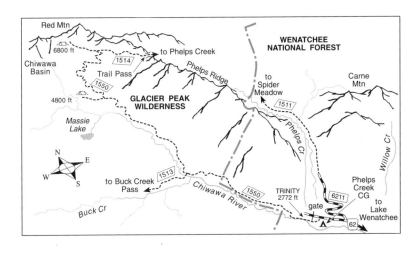

73 CARNE MOUNTAIN

Round trip 7 miles
Hiking time 7 hours
High point 7085 feet
Elevation gain 3585 feet
Hikable July through October

One day or backpack
Map: Green Trails No. 113 Holden
Current information: Ask at Lake
Wenatchee Ranger Station
about trail Nos. 1508 and 1509

Loll around an enchanting basin, enjoying the hideaway seclusion among soaring peaks. Then climb to the summit of Carne Mountain and gaze to the dark summit of mighty Mt. Maude, empress of the Entiat Mountains, and around to Spider Meadow, Red Mountain, Glacier Peak, Ten Peak Mountain, and Mt. Rainier.

Drive the Chiwawa River road (Hike 66) some 22.5 miles from Chiwawa Loop Road (county road No. 22) and turn right on road No. 6211, the Phelps Creek road. Go 2.4 miles to a gate and the trailhead, elevation 3500 feet.

Begin with a scant ¼ mile on the Phelps Creek trail, then turn uphill on Carne Mountain trail No. 1508, ascending a very steep slope through open forest. After the first mile occasional windows open west to the impressive massif of Chiwawa Ridge. Forest eventually is left below, and broad vistas commence. At 2½ miles is a marginal campsite, water supplied by the creek from Carne Basin, which is entered at 3 miles. The greenery of the 6100-foot floor is boxed in by rocky ridges from Carne Mountain. Camps are plentiful in the lovely alpine meadows, though some are horsey and all, in season, are quite buggy. The basin boasts one of the world's largest subalpine larches, which reminds us that in October the forests hereabout turn golden and the bugs have all bugged out to California for the winter.

The trail disappears in the meadow and reappears as the ascent resumes on the far side. At 3½ miles the Carne Mountain trail splits in

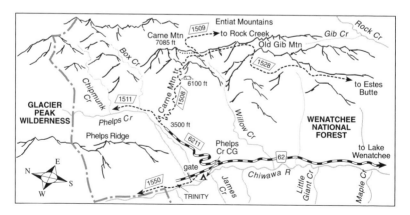

Mount Maude from Carne Mountain (photo by Kirkendall/Spring)

two. The right fork, Old Gib trail No. 1528, climbs to a nearby saddle, 6500 feet, and views of the north face of Old Gib Mountain, then heads south to Estes Butte (Hike 69) and the Chiwawa River road, reached at Rock Creek.

Take the left fork, Rock Creek trail No. 1509, passing at the first switchback a steep but inviting sidetrail to the former site of a fire lookout atop Peak 6991. Continue on the full ¾ mile to a delightful open saddle with a view of the Rock Creek valley, the Entiat Mountains, and awesome Mt. Maude.

The peak-grabbers should go left (north) and follow the footsteps of other peak-grabbers to the 7085-foot summit of Carne Mountain. The view is not really better at the top—it just seems that way.

74 SPIDER MEADOW

**Round trip to upper Spider
Meadow 12½ miles
Hiking time 8 hours
High point 5100 feet
Elevation gain 1700 feet
Hikable mid-July through October**

**One day or backpack
Map: Green Trails No. 113 Holden
Current information: Ask at Lake
Wenatchee Ranger Station
about trail No. 1511**

A glorious valley-bottom meadow in a seeming cul-de-sac amid rugged peaks. Yet the trail ingeniously breaks through the cliffs and climbs to a little "glacier" and a grand overlook of Lyman Basin and summits of the Cascade Crest. For hikers trained in use of the ice ax this can be merely the beginning of a long and classic loop trip described in Hike 75.

Drive the Chiwawa River and Phelps Creek roads (Hike 73) to Phelps Creek trail No. 1511, elevation 3500 feet.

Spider Meadow

The walk begins past the gate on the road, which is still used by miners (as they like to think themselves) almost to the wilderness boundary. The gentle grade goes up and down in forest, passing the Carne Mountain trail in ¼ mile, Box Creek in 1 mile, Chipmunk Creek in 1¾ miles, and the Glacier Peak Wilderness boundary in 2⅔ miles. At 3½ miles, 4175 feet, are the crossing of Leroy Creek, the junction with Leroy Creek trail, a campsite, and the end of the old road.

The way continues through forest interspersed with flower gardens. At 5¼ miles, 4700 feet, is the spectacular opening-out into Spider Meadow; here are good camps. Red Mountain shows its cliffs and snows; the views include other walls enclosing Phelps headwaters—no way can be seen to escape the valley, an apparent dead-end. A mile of flower-walking leads to the crossing of Phelps Creek, 6¼ miles, 5100 feet. A bit beyond are ruins of Ed Linston's cabin. Find good camps here, too. Hikers with only a day or a weekend may turn back, content.

But there is much more, including more good camps. Follow the trail through the meadow, boulder-hop Phelps Creek, and proceed upward. At 6½ miles, 5300 feet, is a junction. The right fork follows Phelps Creek to more meadows and the end of the valley under Dumbell Mountain.

The left fork is a steep, hot, and very dry miners' trail climbing 1100 feet to the lower end of Spider Glacier at 6400 feet. Here are several tiny but spectacular campsites. There's no wood but lots of water and lots of views downvalley to Spider Meadow, Mt. Maude, and Seven-Fingered Jack.

Immediately above is the narrow snowfield of Spider Glacier. In a short mile, either up the snow-filled gully or along the easy and scenic rock spur to the east, is 7100-foot Spider Gap. Look down to the Lyman Glacier, the ice-devastated upper Lyman Basin, and the greenery of the lower basin.

An old trail ascends ¼ mile from the pass to a mine tunnel. One must marvel at the dogged energy of Ed Linston, who hauled machinery and supplies to so airy a spot. After being badly injured by a dynamite explosion in the mine, he was helped down the mountain by his brother. He recovered to spend many more years roaming the Cascades, passing away in 1969 at the age of 82.

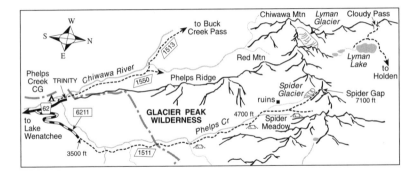

75 SPIDER GAP– BUCK CREEK PASS LOOP

Loop trip 44 miles including Image Lake
Allow 4–7 days
High point 7100 feet
Elevation gain 7200 feet
Hikable late July to late September
Map: Green Trails No. 113 Holden

Current information: Ask at Lake Wenatchee Ranger Station about trail Nos. 1511, 1513, and 1550; Chelan Ranger Station about trail No. 1256; and Darrington Ranger Station about trail Nos. 789 and 2000

Valley-bottom meadows, ridge-crest meadows, tumbling streams, quiet lakes, crags and glaciers—the supreme sampler of the Glacier Peak Wilderness. Don't you dare so much as think of doing it as a cock-a-doodle-doo marathon. The ups, the downs, the torrents for wading, the snows for boot-kicking could permanently squash the swiftness of an overweening ego. Besides, only a loonie would travel such country on the run. The flowers! The sunsets! The blueberries! If your feet twitch for fast action, expend spare energy on off-trail explorations. Take your time. Lots of it. Learn the difference between getting there and being there. Experience the starry nights as well as the sunny (or whatever) days. Choice campsites abound, but mostly in high country where the little inflammable wood that exists is part of the scenery; carry a stove.

The loop can be done in either direction. However, because the snowfield at Spider Gap may be unreasonably dangerous, counterclockwise is recommended in order to keep open a safe line of retreat if the party would rather live than be unreasonable.

Drive the Chiwawa River road, then the Phelps Creek road (Hike 73) to a gate and trailhead, elevation 3500 feet.

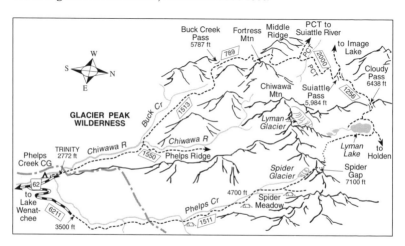

Lyman Glacier and icebergs in Upper Lyman Lakes

Walk past the locked gate on Phelps Creek trail No. 1511 to the Glacier Peak Wilderness at 2.7 miles, Spider Meadow at 5 miles, and Spider Gap at 7100 feet (Hike 74), the highest point of the trip.

An unmaintained path, often buried in snow, descends to Upper Lyman Lake. If the snow is hard and no safe detour is apparent, *turn back* and choose another trip. Your family and friends will thank you, Mountain Rescue will thank you—only the show-biz press will be disappointed.

The three Upper Lyman Lakes are fed by the Lyman Glacier, a stone's throw away, a priceless opportunity to have your photo taken throwing snowballs in August. The unmaintained path drops to forest and Lyman Lake, 5587 feet, some 13 miles from the Phelps Creek gate.

The next stage of the loop climbs to meadows of Cloudy Pass (sidetrip toward North Star Mountain), and at 2.5 miles from Lyman Lake joins the Pacific Crest Trail at Suiattle Pass, 5984 feet. Glacier Peak will pop your eyes here, the first of many times it will do so. A scant ½ mile from the pass the Crest Trail comes to a junction where the loop goes left—but a sidetrip to the right is mandatory, a 7-mile round trip to Image Lake (Hike 12).

Back on the loop, follow the Crest Trail a long 1½ miles, and turn left on trail No. 789, dropping to a crossing of Miners Creek. Having lost 1000 feet to get down in this forest hole, gain it all back climbing to meadows of Middle Ridge—and there's Glacier Peak again, right in the kisser. Descend a bit again, to Small Creek, and climb a bit again, past Flower Dome (yes, Glacier Peak once more bigger than ever) to Buck Creek Pass, 5787 feet.

More sidetrips (Hike 71), a final goodbye to Glacier Peak, and the loop concludes in a 9½-mile descent to Trinity and (sob!) the 2½-mile walk up Phelps Creek road to the car.

76 MAD RIVER–BLUE CREEK CAMPGROUND–MAD LAKE

**Round trip to Blue Creek Camp-
ground 12 miles
Allow 2 days
High point 5400 feet
Elevation gain 1100 feet**

**Round trip from Maverick Saddle
to Mad Lake 16 miles
Allow 2 days
High point 5800 feet
Elevation gain 1550 feet**

**Hikable July to mid-October
Map: Green Trails No. 146 Plain
Current information: Ask at Entiat Ranger Station about trail No. 1409**

The Mad River country of the Entiat Mountains offers miles and
miles of easy, pleasant, family-style roaming. Trails follow noisy creeks
through picturesque glades, trails cross broad meadows of brilliant
flowers, trails round shores of little lakes, and trails climb mountains.
This and the other hikes described here offer a wealth of fun and peace
for a weekend or for a week-long vacation to be enjoyed by old and very
young alike. Tragically, the Forest Service has dedicated the trails to
motorcycles and is reconstructing and relocating routes to permit
higher (noisier) speeds, deliberately converting trails to motorcycle ex-
pressways. That's the bad (dreadful) news. The good news is: motorcycle use is moderate on weekends and virtually zero on weekdays;
wheels (and horses too) are restricted until the trails dry out, generally
July 15th, leaving a small window between melting of enough snow to
permit hiking and the onslaught of the motors. Motorcyclists seldom
camp, so peace comes to backpackers at sunset.

Drive to Coles Corner, between Leavenworth and Stevens Pass, and
north passing Lake Wenatchee State Park. Just beyond the Wenatchee
River bridge go straight ahead on Chiwawa Loop Road. Cross the
Chiwawa River at 3.7 miles. At 4.2 miles, (just beyond Thousand Trails'
sports facilities), turn sharp left on (unsigned) road No. 6100. In another
1.6 miles, at Deep Creek Campground, go right on road No. 6101, signed

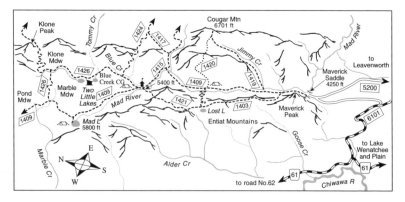

"Maverick Saddle." At 0.4 mile from Deep Creek, stay straight. At 3.2 miles turn right at a hunters' camp. After a final steep and narrow 2 miles only a 4x4 could love is Maverick Saddle 6.1 miles from Deep Creek. To the left is an even rougher road, probably best walked, down 0.3 mile to the start of Mad River trail No. 1409, elevation 4250 feet.

The upriver trail is your way to go. In 1 mile cross a bridge over the Mad River—at this point really just a pretty creek. At 1½ miles is the Jimmy Creek trail, first of three routes to the summit of 6701-foot Cougar Mountain (Hike 77). At 3 miles is an intersection with a trail that goes right to the top of Cougar, left to Lost Lake. At 4 miles cross the Mad River on a log and at 4½ miles recross near a junction with Tyee Ridge trail No. 1415, the third way up Cougar. At 5 miles is a broad meadow and at 5½ miles, 5400 feet, Blue Creek Campground, a splendid spot for the family to spread gear in the open campground or a secluded nook and set out on ramblings. The guard station located here is the last remains of the Mad River Dude Ranch, a popular resort in the late 1920s. The cookhouse stood near the present campground. The blacksmith shop and other buildings were scattered about.

The first ramble, of course, is to continue on the Mad River trail through a series of meadows. At 2 miles from Blue Creek Campground (8 miles from the road) go left on a scant ¼-mile trail to Mad Lake, 5800 feet. On the west shore are excellent camps with water from the inlet stream. As is true of most lakes hereabouts, this one is so silted in that the bottom is too mucky for wading. However, the inlet stream has deposited enough sand to make a semi-solid beach suitable for cooling the feet.

A mandatory sidetrip is the romp through glorious views along the last 2 miles of the Alder Ridge trail.

Early morning at Mad Lake

77 COUGAR MOUNTAIN

Round trip 11 miles
Hiking time 6 hours
High point 6701 feet
Elevation gain 2500 feet
Hikable mid-June through
  October

One day
Map: Green Trails No. 146 Plain
Current information: Ask at
  Entiat Ranger Station about
  trail Nos. 1409, 1419, 1418, and
  1415

It's a stiff climb to the top of Cougar Mountain, but the panoramas from the old lookout site extend from Mt. Rainier to Glacier Peak and out over miles of the 1994 forest fire that stopped just short of the summit. The rock gardens also are worth the effort, especially when

Cougar Mountain after early fall snowstorm. Glacier Peak in distance.

the snow has just melted away in late June or early July and the very stones seem to burst into bloom. The trip can be done as a sortie from a backpack base at Blue Creek Campground (Hike 76) or, as described here, a 1-day jaunt from the Maverick Saddle trailhead.

Drive to Maverick Saddle (Hike 76), elevation 4250 feet.

The start is 1½ miles from the trailhead on Mad River trail No. 1409. A bit past the Mad River crossing, turn right on Jimmy Creek trail No. 1419, gaining 1400 feet in 2½ miles to join abandoned trail No. 1420. Keep right for ½ mile, contouring past a junction with Cougar Ridge trail No. 1418, to a junction with trail No. 1415. Turn left, climbing 500 feet, and fold out the forest map on the sky-surrounded summit, 6701 feet, at 5½ miles from the road.

The trail escaped the forest fire of 1994, which swept up the north and east slopes of Cougar Mountain, creating an interesting contrast to watch the next 100 years.

Cliffs on Cougar Mountain

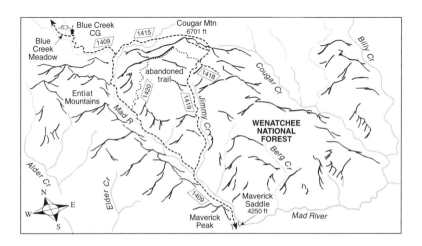

78 WHISTLING PIG LOOP

Loop trip from Blue Creek Campground 6 miles
Hiking time 4 hours
High point 6100 feet
Elevation gain 900 feet
Hikable July to mid-October

One day
Map: Green Trails No. 146 Plain
Current information: Ask at Entiat Ranger Station about trail Nos. 1409, 1415, 1417, 1424, and 1426

A huge meadow and views across the Entiat River valley are the botanical and scenic rewards. The spice of history is provided by an ancient log cabin. As for wildlife, listen for the whistling of the pigs, as the old mountain men called marmots. This trip makes an excellent day trip from Blue Creek Campground, but it can also be a 15-mile loop from Maverick Saddle.

From Blue Creek Campground (Hike 76), elevation 5400 feet, hike Mad River trail No. 1409 downstream toward Maverick Saddle. In 1¼ miles, at 5200 feet, lowest point on the loop, turn left on Tyee Ridge trail No. 1415.

The trail climbs steadily ¾ mile and splits. Straight ahead is the way to Cougar Mountain (Hike 77). Go left on Hunters trail No. 1417 the ½ mile (2½ miles from Blue Creek Campground) to the edge of Whistling Pig Meadow, 5700 feet. Cross to a large grove of trees, site of the old log cabin and the campsites.

The trail enters forest and intersects Middle Tommy Creek trail No. 1424 at 5900 feet. Turn left, contouring a steep hillside to a high point at 6100 feet. Near here spot a naked knoll to the right; leave the trail and climb a short bit to the edge of a cliff and views to mountains across the Entiat valley.

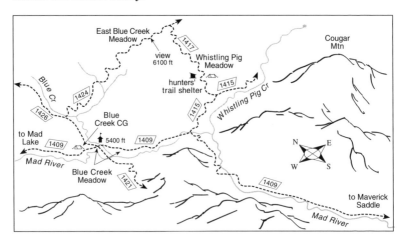

The slope of the hillside gentles out and the trail descends into the Blue Creek drainage, passing East Blue Creek Meadow. At 5½ miles from the start turn left on Blue Creek trail No. 1426 and return to Blue Creek Campground at 6 miles.

Whistling Pig Meadow

79 KLONE PEAK LOOP

Loop trip from Blue Creek Camp-
ground 11½ miles (from
Maverick Saddle 20½ miles)
Hiking time 6 hours
High point 6820 feet
Elevation gain 1500 feet
Hikable July through September

One day
Map: Green Trails No. 146 Plain
Current information: Ask at
Entiat Ranger Station about
trail Nos. 1425, 1427, 1426, and
1409

One of the two lookout cabins that once watched over Mad River country stood atop Klone Peak, 6820 feet. The cabin is gone but the panoramas are as grand as ever: forest, mountains, and even, on the far horizon, the Columbia River Plateau. The meadows along the way are, in themselves, sufficient reason to do what is, after all, not so terribly strenuous a walk, though long.

From Blue Creek Campground (Hike 76), elevation 5400 feet, hike Blue Creek trail No. 1426 the 2 miles to Two Little Lakes and drop a

Klone Peak

hundred feet to a crossing of Tommy Creek, 5400 feet. The forested way is now all up, some stretches steep, some of the switchbacks ridiculously flat, built that way to try to reduce motorcycle and horse erosion in the soft soil of Glacier Peak pumice. At 6200 feet, 4 miles from the campsite, is a junction with North Tommy Ridge trail No. 1425 (Hike 81). Numbers on an old sign here may not be the same as on the new Forest Service map.

Turn right on trail No. 1425, past small waterfalls, and in 1¼ miles turn left on Klone Peak trail No. 1427 a short distance to the summit of Klone Peak, 5½ miles from Blue Creek Campground. To the north are Glacier Peak, Clark Mountain, and Ten Peak. East are Duncan Hill and Pyramid Mountain. South is farm country. Southwest is Mt. Stuart and a tiny bit of Mt. Rainier.

To complete the loop, go 1½ miles back to Blue Creek trail No.

Old guard station near Blue Creek Campground

1426 and turn right, mostly through woods, 1 mile to a junction in Marble Meadows with Mad River trail No. 1409. Turn right 1 mile to the Mad Lake trail, a mandatory sidetrip, ¼ mile each way (Hike 76). Proceed in a succession of meadows to Blue Creek Campground, for a total of 11½ miles.

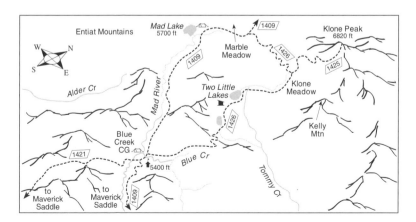

Marble Meadows

CHIWAWA RIVER
Unprotected area

 ENTIAT MOUNTAINS VIEW

Round trip from Maverick Saddle
  25 miles
Allow 2 days
High point 6500 feet
Elevation gain 2500 feet

Hikable July to early October
Map: Green Trails No. 146 Plain
Current information: Ask at
  Entiat Ranger Station
  about trail Nos. 1409 and 1408

No single spectacle makes this trip notable. All it has to offer is miles and miles of meadows rich in flowers and a series of pretty little creeks—and at the end, a view in one direction over the Chiwawa valley to Glacier Peak, in the other down to the depths of the Entiat valley. The length of the trail rules out short-legged hikers. The fact that only the last ½ mile is ORV-free means you must keep a tight rein on your temper.

Each time a bone-headed motorcyclist uses these green lawns to make speed runs and the tight little circles that wheels love to gouge, the ORV Patrol brings rakes and removes the tracks. The majority of ORV riders are responsible (if esthetically myopic) people; only a fraction are outright hooligans. However, not many fools and vandals are required to devastate fragile subalpine terrain; the wounds in the soft soil of Glacier Peak's fields of pumice will remain long after the ecocriminals have gone to their reward. But let not hikers be holier than thou; feet are nowhere near so ruinous as wheels, but they can contribute to the problem. Except for very good reason, always stay on trails.

Drive to Maverick Saddle (Hike 76), elevation 4250 feet.

Hike Mad River trail No. 1409 the 5½ miles to Blue Creek Campground and a junction. Go straight ahead on the Mad River trail, pass the sidetrail to Mad Lake at 8 miles, and at 9 miles intersect trail No. 1426 (Hike 79). Continue straight ahead on the Mad River trail, past Marble Meadow, to a junction with trail No. 1409.2, coming from Chikamin Ridge. Keep straight ahead, past Pond Meadow, into the headwaters of Three Creek. To this point there are a number of wayside camps with plenty of water.

Stay on the Mad River trail, which loses 200 feet, contours, and climbs again. At about 10½ miles cross a small stream on a steep slope. Several switchbacks farther along pass a small meadow, then a larger one, the same stream flowing through them. This is the only camp with year-round water for the next 9 miles.

The trail climbs to 6200 feet, drops 100 feet, and again climbs. At 12 miles, 6300 feet, are a junction with the Shetipo trail, the official end of the Mad River trail, and the legal stopping point for motorcycles (heh! heh!). Your way continues straight ahead on what now is Garland Peak trail No. 1408 (Hike 86), becoming very steep, then leveling off to a first look at Glacier Peak, screened by trees. Leave the trail and walk up the 6643-foot knoll for the promised views.

You needn't stop here, of course. The viewpoint is merely the first such along the crest of the Entiat Mountains into the Glacier Peak Wilderness. The next year-round water is 7 miles farther on, at Cow Creek Pass. Beyond it are Larch Lakes at 9 miles, Pomas Pass at 15, and the trail-end at the junction with Ice Creek trail, 17 miles from the 6500-foot viewpoint.

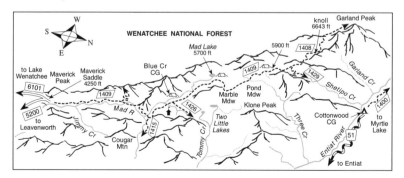

81 NORTH TOMMY RIDGE

Round trip 13 miles
Hiking time 7 hours
High point 6820 feet
Elevation gain 2900 feet in,
500 feet out
Hikable July through October

One day
Map: Green Trails No. 146 Plain
Current information: Ask at
Entiat Ranger Station about
trail No. 1425

Each of five high points on North Tommy Ridge has grand panoramas of mountains and farms and makes a satisfying turnaround. Of course, the farthest and highest (the old fire-lookout site atop Klone Peak) is the bestest.

Until 1986 the second mile of this trail was extremely rough, steep, and difficult. Consequently, the route was seldom used by motorcycles and ORVs; the few that did dug deep into the soft pumice soil, instituting drainage channels that snowmelt trenched knee-deep, utterly destroying long stretches of tread. Rather than recognize that pumice country is no place for high-speed wheels, the Forest Service obtained $87,776 of our Washington State gas-tax money to reconstruct the trail to motorcycle standards. The soft, light soil required the motorcycle trail (expressway) to be built at the 10-percent grade abhorred by hikers; endless switchbacks that even go downhill before turning up will invite shortcuts which become erosion channels. The switchbacks are banked and hardened with concrete blocks so the wheels won't have to slow down. A trail once almost machine-free has become a motorcycle obstacle course (with you, the hiker, as the obstacle). The cheapest and simplest answer to the damage of the past would have been to spend a

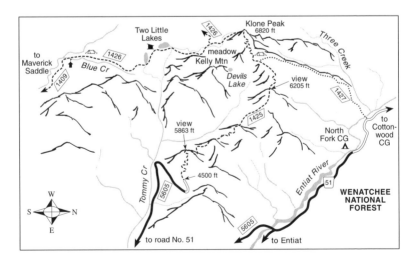

View from first high point on North Tommy Ridge

few hundred dollars to fill the worst of the ruts, put in short stretches of new tread, and prohibit the machines that were ripping up the country. However the motorcyclists persuaded the Forest Service, which never so much as gave hikers a chance to say "NO."

From Entiat drive 30.8 miles on the Entiat River road and turn left on road No. 5605, signed "North Tommy Trail." In 7 miles reach the road-end and North Tommy trail No. 1425, elevation 4500 feet.

The first ¼ mile is on an abandoned road. The next mile gains a mere 100 feet to a creek crossing, the only water on the route. Then begins the 10-percent monotony. At 3 miles is the top of the first knoll, 5863 feet, with views from a helipad clearing.

The trail drops 300 feet, climbs 600 feet to the second knoll, loses a bit and gains 100 feet to the third, loses 100 feet and gains 200 to the fourth. You can't quit now.

The path drops 200 feet to a junction with the abandoned Klone Peak trail from the Entiat valley (Hike 82), loses 100 feet along a narrow ridge crest, and bumps against the base of Klone Peak. Climb a final 600 feet, to within a few hundred feet of the summit, and join the Blue Creek trail, a popular route from the Mad River trail. At 6½ miles from the road step out on the lastest and bestest panorama point. The USGS map says the summit is 6820 feet; the sign on top says 6834. The cabin was destroyed by vandals in 1959, but the foundation is still there. So are the views.

82 OLD KLONE PEAK TRAIL

Round trip 10 miles
Hiking time 7 hours
High point 6820 feet
Elevation gain 4000 feet
Hikable July through September
One day

Map: Green Trails No. 146 Plain
  (not on map)
Current information: Ask at
  Entiat Ranger Station about
  trail No. 1426

Would you like to reach all that good stuff on Tommy Ridge (Hike 80) with no hassle by machines? This abandoned trail is for you. While struggling over the blowdowns, bless the Forest Service for letting this trail stay motor-free in an area overrun by gas-guzzlers, smoke-poopers, and ditch-gougers. The benefaction didn't cost a nickel of public funds. Nature installed the wheelstops, at no charge. So much for the good news. The bad news is the necessity to cross the Entiat River sans bridge and then to gain 4000 feet of altitude.

From Entiat drive 35.4 miles on the Entiat River road to Three Creek Campground, elevation 2900 feet. In early summer the Entiat River is too deep and swift to ford but in late summer is only knee deep. Some years a logjam or fallen tree spans the flood, so check between Three Creek Campground and downstream as far as Spruce Campground. Once across intersect the long abandoned Three Creek trail and head downstream. Cut logs give a good indication of the trail's location.

Signpost on old Klone Peak trail

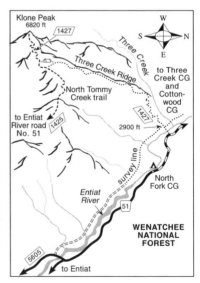

If there is no logjam, no safe wade, drive to road No. 5605. Cross the river on a concrete bridge and in 0.1 mile go right on road No. (5605)125 for 2.5 miles to its end in a clearcut, elevation 2300 feet. Follow, if you can, a line of Survey ribbons upstream 1 long mile to the Klone Peak trail close to Three Creek.

The trail sticks close to Three Creek for a scant ½ mile, then switchbacks away; tread thins to nothing at the critical point—scout around for cutbanks and cut logs. The story from here is switchbacks, 3500 feet gained in 3½ miles, on a broad hillside that narrows to a thin ridge. Holes open in the forest, giving a good look at Pyramid Mountain and, at the ridge top, a glimpse of Glacier Peak. A short drop leads to a junction with North Tommy trail No. 1425 (Hike 81), 6300 feet, 4 miles from the river. Join the motorcycles for the final short ascent to the top of Klone Peak, 6820 feet.

Near the North Tommy junction are campsites, but no water after the snow melts. Carry a gallon.

A lucky windfall over Entiat River

83 THREE CREEK TRAIL

Round trip to high point 13 miles
Hiking time 10 hours
High point 6569 feet
Elevation gain 4300 feet

Loop trip 17 miles
Hiking time 12 hours
High point 6569 feet
Elevation gain 4500 feet

Hikable late June through October
One day or backpack
Map: Green Trails No. 146 Plain (trail not shown)
Current information: Ask at Entiat Ranger Station about trail No. 1428

Actually, the Three Creek trail is never close to the creek.

The easy ways to the lovely meadows of the upper Mad River area have all been usurped by motorcycle riders. The integrity of only two long, abandoned trails—the original Klone Peak trail (Hike 82) and the Three Creek trail described here—has been preserved, and not by any

Three Creek trail

possible Forest Service sense of justice, but by numerous windfalls, thus giving motor-free access to the Mad River meadows. Hikers are trying to obtain "Hiker-Only" status for the two abandoned trails, after which volunteers will cut out the windfalls. Even then, the 4300-foot elevation gain will be no stroll. For an older or a child, the Mad River ORV speedway (Hike 76) still will be the only way.

Drive the Entiat River road some 35.4 miles to Three Creek Campground, elevation 2900 feet, and get across by one of the three alternatives described in Hike 82.

Across the Entiat River locate the long-abandoned trail. In the virgin forest cut logs and cut banks give a good indication of the trail's location. Directly opposite from the campground the Three Creek trail makes an abrupt 90-degree turn and heads uphill.

The way gains elevation rapidly as it makes a mile-long traverse of Three Creek Ridge to the first of many switchbacks at 3400 feet.

Windfalls on the steep hillsides are often difficult. While some are easily stepped over, others are real obstacles that must be crowded under, climbed over, or detoured around. Don't whine—this is all that keeps the motorcycles out. The way pushes upward with only an occasional narrow window toward Klone Peak or down onto the Entiat River bottom. The trail stays in forest most of the way, a blessing on a hot day. Views don't open up until the last ½ mile. At about 5 miles cross a tributary of Three Creek and a possible campsite. At 6½ miles reach the 6569-foot high point and a good turnaround point.

For a loop, continue on another mile and go left on Mad River trail No. 1409 and put up with motorcycle traffic for a long mile. Then go left again toward Klone Peak on trail No. 1426, trail No. 1427, and finally on trail No. 1425 going over the top of Klone Peak and down the motor-abandoned Klone Peak trail described in Hike 82.

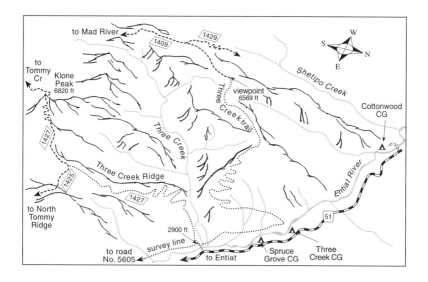

84 DUNCAN HILL

Round trip from road No. 2920
14 miles
Hiking time 7 hours
High point 7819 feet
Elevation gain 3300 feet

Round trip via Anthem Creek
trail 16½ miles
Hiking time 12 hours
High point 7819 feet
Elevation gain 4700 feet

Hikable mid-July through mid-October
One day or backpack
Map: Green Trails No. 114 Lucerne
Current information: Ask at Entiat Ranger Station about trail Nos.
1434, 1435, and 1400

Sweat and pant and grumble to a former lookout site atop 7819-foot
Duncan Hill, and there be richly rewarded for the suffering with views
up and down the Entiat valley, from golden sagebrush hills to the rock-
and-snow giants of Mt. Maude and Seven-Fingered Jack. The trail
traverses the peak, making possible two quite different routes that can
be combined in a superb loop, if transportation can be arranged from
one trailhead to another. It is also the opening leg of another fine loop
to Milham Pass. To ameliorate the suffering, carry water to compensate for Nature's stinginess.

According to the Forest Service ranger, except during hunting season this trail is so little used by machines or feet you can have a purer
wilderness experience here than on the Entiat River trail. However,
the soft pumice of the Duncan Hill trail has been so sorely grooved by a
few motorbike wheels that one must often walk to the side of the ruined tread.

From Entiat on the Columbia River drive the Entiat River road 33
miles (5 miles short of the end at Cottonwood Campground), and near
North Fork Campground turn right on road No. 5608. At 5.8 miles
(dodging lesser sideroads) stay right at a well-traveled intersection and
at 6 miles go left a short distance to trail No. 1434, elevation 5200 feet.

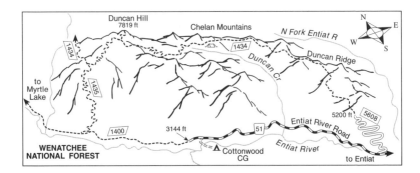

Glacier Peak from Duncan Hill

The way sets out along wooded Duncan Ridge, climbing a 5549-foot knob, dropping 100 feet, then climbing again to 5800 feet. The grade moderates and in about 3½ miles enters semi-meadows, with water and good camps, at the head of Duncan Creek. At about 5 miles is a junction; keep right. At 6½ miles is another junction; again keep right and climb to the top of 7819-foot Duncan Hill and its solar-powered radio, 7 miles from the road.

For the second approach, drive all the 38 miles to Cottonwood Campground, elevation 3144 feet. Try this route in May or June. There likely will be too much snow to reach the summit, but the spring flowers and the abundance of does with fawns are worth it. (Look at and photograph them all you want, but never touch.)

Walk Entiat River trail No. 1400 a flattish 2½ miles and turn right, uphill, on Anthem Creek trail No. 1435. Now the fun begins—if your idea of entertainment is endless switchbacks gaining 2400 feet. At 5900 feet, 6 miles from the road, is the junction with Duncan Ridge trail No. 1434. For camping, turn left ¼ mile to water or 1 mile farther to a spot about 500 feet above the crossing of Anthem Creek. For the summit, turn right and climb open scree and flowers; the tread becomes obscure, so watch it. At 7¾ miles is a junction; take the upper trail to the summit, 8¼ miles.

If a party has two cars, or some other ingenious scheme, the two summit approaches make a dandy combination.

For a loop of famous flowers and views, at the 5900-foot junction turn left on Duncan Ridge trail the 6 up-and-down miles to Snowbrushy Creek trail and Milham Pass (Hike 97). Descend to the Entiat River trail and then the road.

85 MYRTLE LAKE

Round trip 8½ miles
Hiking time 4 hours
High point 3765 feet
Elevation gain 600 feet
Hikable mid-June through
October

One day or backpack
Map: Green Trails No. 114
Lucerne
Current information: Ask at
Entiat Ranger Station about
trail Nos. 1400 and 1404

Deep forest of the lower Entiat valley provides an ambling entry to the jade-green lake hidden in a fold of ridges falling from Rampart Mountain. The trail grade is easy, the camping is pleasant, the swimming is bracing. Of all the hikes in the Entiat, this is the ideal trail for a family with small children. Children? Make sure they look both ways before stepping out on the trail. The Forest Service has made it into a motorcycle track and now there are swarms of fat-tire bicycles.

From Entiat drive the Entiat River road 38 miles to its end, 0.4 mile beyond Cottonwood Camp, elevation 3144 feet.

Hike Entiat River trail No. 1400 through deep forest, distant from the river. Note that as a pedestrian you are a third-class citizen. The trail has been widened for motorcycles and a swath cut through the shade trees to accommodate horses' hips; the walker must sweat in the hot sun.

In 2½ miles, minor ups and downs netting a mere 400 feet, pass Anthem Creek trail No. 1435 and, in ¼ mile more, a sylvan camp at Anthem Creek. Note the wide bridge; before the trail was reconstructed for motorcycles a footlog did the job. The Forest Service has to abandon foot trails for lack of funds, but there's no shortage of money to speed the wheels.

The way pokes along the valley floor, the forest opening here and there for glimpses of Devil's Smoke Stack and Rampart Mountain. At 3½ miles turn left on Cow Creek-Myrtle Lake trail No. 1404 and cross the river on a bridge. In a couple hundred yards the trail splits. Both forks climb, at a slightly steeper pitch, to Myrtle Lake, 3700 feet. For camping take the left fork, which

Deer on Entiat River trail

Myrtle Lake

rounds the shore to peaceful forest sites at the south end (wheels are banned). For day-hiking take the right fork to the north end of the lake. Gaze upon the serene waters in the lovely forest bowl, greenery interrupted only by cliffs and talus on the west side.

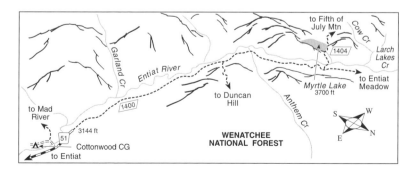

86 DEVIL'S SMOKE STACK LOOP

Loop trip 22¾ miles	**Maps: Green Trails No. 114**
Allow 2–3 days	**Lucerne and No. 146 Plain**
High point 7400 feet	**Current information: Ask at**
Elevation gain 6254 feet	**Entiat Ranger Station about**
Hikable mid-July through	**trail Nos. 1400, 1404, 1408, and**
September	**1429**

Aside from the intimations of diabolism (the Hell-hued rocks of the volcanic neck thrusting ruggedly through sheer cliffs), this high-country loop has much to daunt the faint heart. The trail is extremely steep in spots and in others next to non-existent. All day you face the barren waste without the taste of water, cool, clear water (water!). After the snow melts, few places on the route have so much as damp grass all summer. On the other hand, for the strong of heart the trail is full of surprises such as flowers blooming on otherwise barren hillsides, colorful rocks, and lots of solitude.

Drive to the end of the Entiat River road (Hike 84), elevation 3144 feet.

Hike to Myrtle Lake, 3700 feet, 4¼ miles (Hike 85). Now the climb begins, switchbacking through deep woods, over a rocky shoulder of Rampart Mountain; a bare knob off the trail to the right gives views to the Entiat valley. The way rounds the corner of the shoulder and eases off, contouring steep walls of the Cow Creek valley. At 2 miles beyond Myrtle Lake, 6¼ miles from the road, a spur trail goes left over a little rise to Cow Creek Meadows, 5100 feet, a large parkland flat enclosed by cliffs of Rampart and Fifth of July Mountains. Campsites are numerous. A virtually permanent heap of avalanche snow yields meaningful water.

Again the uphill labor, ameliorated by splendid cross-Entiat views to

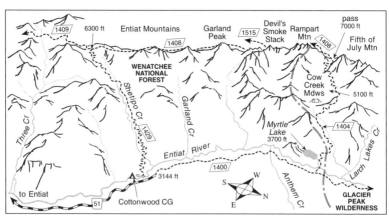

Devil's Smoke Stack from Garland Peak trail

Duncan Hill, Peak 7936, and Gopher Mountain. At 6000 feet the trail passes a terrific viewpoint on a rock buttress, a campsite, and a path to water. Larch forest commences. At 8½ miles from the road, the Cow Creek trail ends by intersecting Garland Peak trail No. 1408, 6600 feet. To the right is a little waterfall creek with several fine camps a short climb above the trail; farther to the right, and down, are the campsites at Larch Lakes (Hike 87), 1½ miles from the intersection.

The loop, however, turns left, abruptly descending a pumice slope, skirting below a band of cliffs, and climbing to Cow Creek Pass (or Fifth of July Pass), 7000 feet, on the shoulder of Fifth of July Mountain. The short scramble to the summit and its commanding views is just about mandatory.

From the shoulder, drop to a 6800-foot saddle; the trail becomes

Shetipo Creek trail

vague to imaginary, the blazes half-a-century old. Turn west, traverse to a long rib, and descend to a basin with a small meadow camp—the Ravens Roost—at 5900 feet. There is water all summer, usually. A long uphill swing around the side of Rampart Mountain, then switchbacks, lead to an old sheepherders' camp. Water sometimes. The trail vanishes, reappears above a clump of trees, and proceeds around Rampart to a narrow saddle, 7100 feet.

The way levels off for a wide-open contour around Devil's Smoke Stack to an exposed knob, 7400 feet, with views to everywhere. This is the highest elevation of the loop. Gaze to your full, then drop the short bit to intersect the Basalt Ridge trail (Hike 66), 13 miles from the start.

The trail sidehills open ground toward Garland Peak, the soil fragile, criss-crossed with confusing animal traces; the correct path climbs briefly, then drops gently as it rounds Garland Peak (Hike 66), another sidetrip essential for view hogs. The way drops, climbs, and drops to a wooded saddle, 6100 feet; a sidetrail leads to Pinto Camp, an agreeable meadow with a very questionable spring.

At 17½ miles the Garland trail ends in a little pass at a junction with Shetipo Creek trail No. 1429, 6300 feet. Motorcycles are permitted to run here; at some corners the tread is rutted so deeply that multiple-use is a difficult feat. Zigging and zagging down 5 long miles, the trail enters Cottonwood Campground on the Entiat River. Cross on the car bridge and find a path heading upriver the final ¼ mile to the parking lot, closing the loop at 22¾ miles.

Weathered wood

87 LARCH LAKES LOOPS

Round trip to Larch Lakes
  13 miles
Hiking time 8 hours
High point 5742 feet
Elevation gain 2600 feet

Loop trip (shorter loop) 18 miles
Allow 2–3 days
High point 6500 feet
Elevation gain 3400 feet

Hikable mid-July through September
Map: Green Trails No. 114 Lucerne
Current information: Ask at Entiat Ranger Station about trail Nos.
  1400, 1430, 1408, and 1404

Amazingly, the two loveliest lakes in the Entiat valley, surrounded by alpine parkland nestled under cliffs of Fifth of July Mountain, get virtually no company. Indeed, neither do the miles and miles of up-and-down high trails along the Entiat Mountains to which they are the entryway.

Drive to the end of the Entiat River road (Hike 84), elevation 3144 feet.

Hike Entiat River trail No. 1400 for 3½ miles and go left on Cow Creek trail No. 1404. A short ⅓ mile past Myrtle Lake go right on Larch Lakes hiker-only trail No. 1430. The way contours to the horse trail and then begins a grueling climb of 1900 feet in 2½ miles, switchbacking up a treeless, shadeless, waterless south slope. On a hot day the best plan is to loiter by Myrtle Lake until late afternoon, when sun has left the hillside—or better yet, cook dinner at the lake and make the ascent in the cool of the evening. Waiting until morning does no good; the hillside gets the first rays of sun.

Before starting up, note the waterfall high on the hillside to the west. Elevation of this falls (which comes from the lake outlet) provides a measure of how much climbing remains to be done.

The tortuous switchbacks abruptly flatten into a traverse along the shores of Lower Larch Lake, leading to a large meadow and acres of flat ground for camping. The trail continues a short ½ mile to Upper Larch Lake, 5700 feet, more meadows, and the junction with the Pomas Creek trail. Here is a choice of loop trips.

For the longer of the two, climb north some 700 feet to Larch Lakes Pass, then amble northward on to 6350-foot Pomas Pass and down Pomas Creek to a junction with the Ice Creek trail, 6 miles from Upper Larch Lake. Go left to Ice Lakes (Hike 88) or right to the Entiat River trail.

For the shorter and more popular loop, follow the trail south around Upper Larch Lake. Tread disappears in meadows and several starts can be seen on the wooded hillside left of Fifth of July Mountain. The correct path goes into the woods at the base of the slope a couple of hundred feet from a granite "island" in the meadow.

Upper Larch Lake

The trail climbs steadily more than a mile, with airy views down to Larch Lakes, then contours the mountain to a 6637-foot junction with the Cow Creek trail, the return route via Myrtle Lake.

The ascent of Fifth of July Mountain is a must. Though the north face of the peak is a tall, rugged cliff, there's an easy side. Leave packs at the junction and climb the Garland Peak trail a mile south to 7000-foot Cow Creek Pass (some signs say Fifth of July Pass) and ascend the gentle south slope to the 7696-foot summit and a 360-degree panorama of Glacier, Clark, Maude, Rainier, and other peaks beyond counting.

The Cow Creek trail descends a steep 2 miles to the edge of Cow Creek Meadows and another 2 miles via Myrtle Lake (Hike 85) to the Entiat River trail, reached at a point 3½ miles from the road-end.

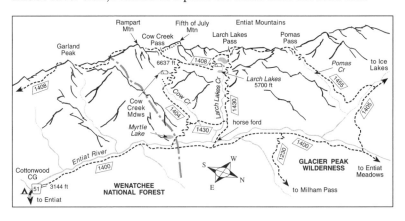

88

ENTIAT MEADOWS AND ICE LAKES

Round trip to Lower Ice Lake
  28 miles
Allow 3–5 days
High point (knoll above lower
  lake) 6900 feet
Elevation gain 4200 feet
Hikable August through
  September

Round trip to Entiat Meadows
  30 miles
Allow 3–4 days or more
High point 5500 feet
Elevation gain 2400 feet
Hikable July through October

Maps: Green Trails No. 114 Lucerne and No. 113 Holden
Current information: Ask at Entiat Ranger Station about trail Nos.
  1400 and 1405

A long trail with many byways to glory and at the two ends a pair of climaxes: a vast meadow under small glaciers hanging on the walls of a row of 9000-foot peaks, and two high, remote lakes set in cirque basins close under cliffs of 9082-foot Mt. Maude, alpine trees standing out starkly in a barren, glaciated landscape reminiscent of Khyber Pass. Mountain goats, too, often stand out in the open.

Drive to the end of the Entiat River road (Hike 84), elevation 3144 feet.

Hike Entiat River trail No. 1400, the first 4½ miles of which were engineered by the Forest Service into a motorcycle expressway which nowadays gets lots of bicycle use but very few motors. At 3½ miles is the turnoff to the Cow Creek trail and Myrtle Lake, destination of most people. At 5 miles is the Larch Lakes horse trail (Hike 87) and at 5½ miles a campsite by Snowbrushy Creek. At 6½ miles, 3900 feet, is a beautiful camp below the trail in Snowbrushy Meadows; here too is the

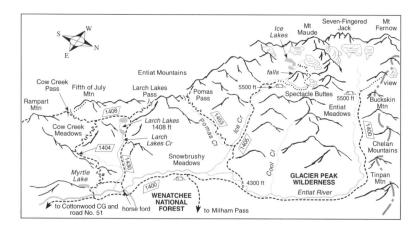

Ice Creek Falls

Snowbrushy Creek trail to Milham Pass (Hike 97). At 8¼ miles, 4300 feet, reach the split.

Ice Lakes: The Ice Creek trail goes left a short bit to a camp and a two-log bridge over the river; if the bridge is missing, look upstream for a log. The way climbs gradually in forest the first mile, then drops 400 feet to Ice Creek. At 1½ miles, 4300 feet, is a junction with the Pomas Creek trail, an excellent alternate return route via Larch Lakes (Hike 87).

The route goes along the river, alternating between small alpine trees and meadows. At about 3 miles is a crossing of Ice Creek; since a footlog seldom is available and the channel is too wide to jump, be prepared to wade—and find out how well the creek lives up to its name. In another mile is another crossing, but this time the creek can be stepped over on rocks. At some 4½ miles from the Entiat trail, formal tread ends in a rocky meadow at a delightful campsite, 5500 feet. The noisy creek drowns the sound of a pretty waterfall tumbling from Upper Ice Lake.

From the trail-end a boot-built path follows the rocky meadow north to the valley head, passing the waterfall. Generally keep right of the creek, but cross to the left when the going looks easier there. The valley ends in a steep, green hillside; above, in hanging cirques, lie the lakes. From a starting point to the right of the creek, scramble up game traces, crossing the creek and climbing between cliffs to its left. The way emerges onto a rocky knoll 100 feet above 6822-foot Lower Ice Lake, 6 miles from the Entiat trail. Camp on pumice barrens, not the fragile heather; no fires permitted.

Upper Ice Lake is a mile farther. Head southwest in a shallow alpine valley, below cliffs, to the outlet stream and follow the waters up to the 7200-foot lake, beautifully cold and desolate.

Mt. Maude cliffs are impressive from the lakes.

Entiat Meadows: The way to the split is principally through forest; the final 7 miles up the Entiat River alternate between trees and meadows. Though sheep have not been allowed in the valley for years,

Entiat Meadows

Lower Ice Lake

some meadows still show deep rutting from thousands of hooves, and some of the native flowers have never grown back.

At 13 miles, having gained only some 2000 feet thus far, the grade steepens a little for a final 1½ miles and then, at about 5500 feet, the tread fades out in fields of heather and flowers. The camps are fine throughout the miles-long Entiat Meadows and the views are grand—up the cliffs of the huge cirque to the summits of Fernow, Seven-Fingered Jack, and Maude, all above 9000 feet, and to remnants of the Entiat Glacier, which in days of glory excavated the cirque and gave the valley its contours.

If ambition persists, scramble up grassy slopes of the ridge to the north and look down into Railroad Creek and the town of Holden.

89 BIG HILL–PYRAMID MOUNTAIN

Round trip 18 miles
Hiking time 10 hours
High point 8243 feet
Elevation gain 3000 feet in,
  1200 feet out
Hikable mid-July to mid-
  September

One day or backpack
Map: Green Trails No. 114
  Lucerne
Current information: Ask at
  Entiat Ranger Station about
  trail Nos. 1433 and 1441

Spectacular, yes, walking a ridge so high it almost touches the sky, looking out through miles of empty air to Glacier Peak, lording it over an infinity of icy-craggy attendants. The supreme moment is standing where once the lookout cabin did, atop Pyramid Mountain, with an airplane-wing view 7000 feet straight down to blue waters of Lake Chelan. However, a word to the thrifty: If the summit of Pyramid is your main goal, you do better to get there via South Pyramid Creek (Hike 93), saving much wear and tear on the family car; the road to Big Hill trailhead varies from so-so to bad to atrocious.

From Highway 97A drive the Entiat River road some 19 miles and turn right on road No. 5900 signed "Lake Chelan," which is often dusty and rutted, always steep and narrow. At 8.4 miles keep left at Shady Pass on road No. (5900)112. At 10.2 miles pass Big Hill. Keep left on road No. (5900)113 to the road-end and trailhead, 10.7 miles from the Entiat, elevation 6458 feet.

Pyramid Mountain trail No. 1433 sets out on a wide firebreak which the fire crews slashed to keep busy while waiting for the rains to come and put out the 1970 Entiat Fire. It climbs around the first bump, passes Poodle Dog Camp, and at about 1½ miles climbs to a 7000-foot high point on Crow Hill. A heartbreaking drop ensues, to 6200 feet. At 3 miles pass the Butte Creek trail and a nice camp at the head of Butte

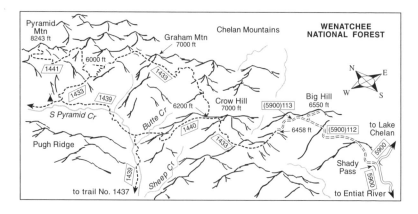

Creek. A gutwrenching climb goes to 7000 feet on flower-meadow Graham Mountain. Again (sob!) a drop to 6000 feet. At 6 miles are a junction and another camp with water. Turn right on Pyramid View trail No. 1441 and at 9 miles step proudly onto the summit of Pyramid Mountain, 8243 feet, and enjoy your promised reward.

Pyramid Mountain trail on side of Crow Hill

90 NORTH FORK ENTIAT RIVER

Round trip to trail-end 16 miles
  (to Fern Lake junction 12 miles)
Allow 2 days
High point 6600 feet
Elevation gain 2600 feet

Hikable late July through October
Map: Green Trails No. 114 Lucerne
Current information: Ask at
  Entiat Ranger Station about
  trail No. 1437

The North Fork Entiat River country has 43 miles of trails offering dramatic views, flower-rich meadows, and loud streams. A great area for beginning hikers who want to enjoy in peace the lovely walks in the low valleys, for intermediates ambitious to take off on a glorious ridge run starting from one of the highest roads in the state, and for experienced highlanders fond of the strenuous climb to an old lookout site. The main thoroughfare is a forest trail passing through several small meadows to a delightful camp beside a little stream with a big name— North Fork Entiat River. Here is a fine base for day hikes.

(Good news about public activism: After years of motorcycles harassing the North Fork trails, 5000 letters—plus a citizens' lawsuit—got the paths returned to hikers.)

From Entiat drive the Entiat River road some 32.5 miles and turn right 4 miles on road No. 5606 to North Fork Entiat trail No. 1437, elevation 4000 feet.

The trail immediately crosses Crow Creek and, after some ups and downs, boulder-hops South Pyramid Creek at 1 mile (but not in early July, it doesn't). At 1½ miles pass the South Pyramid Creek trail (Hike 93) and at 2¾ miles, the Pugh Ridge trail (Hike 91). At about 4 miles small meadows begin to break the forest; come early for the flowers. At 5 miles the trail gets very steep and stays that way to the Fern Lake junction, 5300 feet, 6 miles; here is that delightful camp by the river, the spot to lay out a mountain home.

After 1 more upstream mile the path again tilts very steeply, gaining 1000 feet in ¾ mile. At 8 miles from the road it ends at a junction

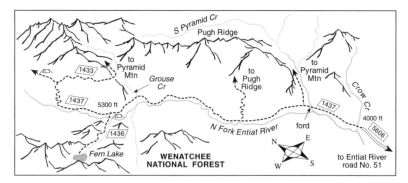

North Fork Entiat River trail

with the Pyramid Mountain trail, 6600 feet. Go left a short bit to a large meadow with fine camps, more mountain homes.

Are your legs still jittering for exercise? Take the Pyramid Mountain trail 2 miles to Saska Pass, 7425 feet, and views down Snowbrushy Creek and the North Fork valley. Or continue down into the South Pyramid Valley for a loop (Hike 94).

91 PUGH RIDGE–PYRAMID CREEK LOOP

Round trip 12 miles to Pugh Ridge
Hiking time 9 hours
Loop trip 14 miles
Hiking time 10 hours
High point 6800 feet
Elevation gain 2800 feet
Hikable July to mid-October

One day
Map: Green Trails No. 114
    Lucerne
Current information: Ask at
    Entiat Ranger Station about
    trail Nos. 1437 and 1438

The close views of the giant peaks of the Chelan Mountains are a joy forever, and they're only part of the scenery. The meadows are very good, too. The trail is rough, at a steep angle. So much the better, giving a degree of solitude.

Drive North Fork Entiat River road No. 5606 (Hike 90) to North Fork Entiat trail No. 1437, elevation 4000 feet.

Hike the North Fork trail 2¾ miles to the Pugh Ridge trail, 4300 feet, and turn right, steeling yourself to gain 2500 feet in 3 miles. The opening ¾ mile switchbacks 800 feet; that average rate of gain is maintained. At 1¼ miles is a nice streamside camp. Nearing timberline the tread grows fainter and in the meadowlands is lost altogether. No matter. Continue up in the open until there is no more up. At 6 miles from the road sit down atop Pugh Ridge at 6800 feet. To the north is the magnificent line of Saska, Emerald, and Cardinal Peaks, all about 8500 feet. East are the naked slopes of Pyramid Mountain (Hike 89). West are the crags of Duncan Hill (Hike 84). In the middle distance is the Devil's Smoke Stack.

For the loop, cross the summit meadow. No tread here so scout out the trail down a bit on the west side, and do not leave the meadow until certain you really have trail underfoot. It drops several hundred

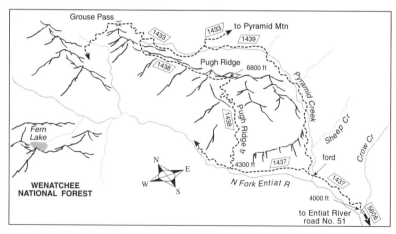

feet, climbs to a 7000-foot high point, and descends to an intersection, 8 miles from the road, with trail No. 1433, called the Pyramid Mountain trail though it never goes to the mountain.

Turn downhill to another intersection. Keep straight, continuing down Pyramid Creek trail No. 1439 (Hike 94) to the North Fork Entiat trail at 1¼ miles from the road, for a loop total of 14 miles.

Meadows on Pugh Ridge

92 FERN LAKE

Round trip 15 miles from road
Allow 2 days
High point 6894 feet
Elevation gain 2800 feet
Hikable mid-July through-
September

Map: Green Trails No. 114
Lucerne
Current information: Ask at
Entiat Ranger Station about
trail Nos. 1437 and 1436

As something of a geological curiosity, Fern Lake is the only lake in North Fork Entiat drainage. Why just this single cirque cupping deep water? Not enough snow in the last few "little ice ages" to crank up the glaciers? The shores might be expected to be a three-deep ring of fishermen. However, the extremely difficult trail (for a mercy, signed "Hiker Only") keeps out the pikers.

Drive to the North Fork Entiat trail No. 1437 (Hike 90), trailhead elevation 4000 feet.

Hike 6 miles to the Fern Creek trail junction, 5300 feet. The camp here is very pleasant and there isn't another spot before the lake to lay your weary bones. The question, therefore, is whether to day-hike from this base or carry packs the 1½ extremely steep miles to the lake, where very few bones can find space.

Cross the North Fork Entiat River—dwindled here to a creek—on an upstream log, and start the switchbacks. Don't complain about the numerous windfalls—they help keep scofflaw horses off this "hiker-only" trail. About halfway up, the trail leaves forest and climbs steeply beside the lake's outlet, tumbling so steeply it's practically all waterfall. The ascent ends abruptly on the shore of the lake, 6800 feet, ringed by ice-scoured cliffs and slabs and buttresses. The little campsite is such a

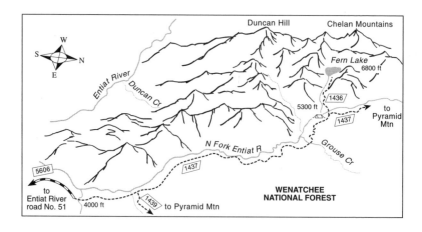

Glacier-smoothed rocks at Fern Lake

joy you'll be sorry if you took the course of prudence and left your overnight gear below. What's a couple of hours of donkey misery beside a
night and morning living in such glory?

93 PYRAMID MOUNTAIN

Round trip 19 miles
Allow 2 days
High point 8243 feet
Elevation gain 4300 feet
Hikable mid-July through
September

Map: Green Trails No. 114
Lucerne
Current information: Ask at
Entiat Ranger Station about
trail Nos. 1437, 1439, 1433,
and 1441

The views from this old lookout site extend over range upon range of snow mountains in the Glacier Peak Wilderness, over heat-hazy plateaus of the Columbia Basin, and straight down 7000 feet to Lake Chelan, so far below that binoculars are needed to spot the *Lady of the Lake*. One has to wonder why the place was chosen for a fire lookout— the scenery is all rock, ice, and water, hardly anything in sight that might burn.

The two ways to Pyramid Mountain are the same length and have about the same elevation gain. The route from Big Hill (Hike 89) is spectacular, but the drive to the trailhead is so long and difficult that the recommended route, described here, is the South Pyramid Creek trail, featuring an interesting transition from valley forest to mountain barren.

Thanks to the period when the Forest Service exuberantly promoted machines and had more money than it knew how to use sensibly, the hiking trail was rebuilt with wide tread; little creeks were provided with big sturdy bridges, and the boulders employed by hikers to cross big creeks were removed to permit wheels to splash through without slowing.

Hike North Fork Entiat trail No. 1437 (Hike 90), trailhead elevation

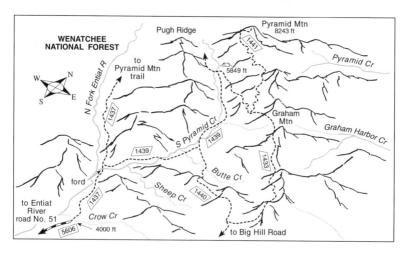

4000 feet. In 1 mile cross Pyramid Creek and at 1¼ miles turn right on South Pyramid Creek trail No. 1439. At 5½ miles, 5849 feet, are the last creekside campsites. At the junction here go right on Pyramid Mountain trail No. 1433, climbing 1¼ miles to another junction; go left here on Pyramid Viewpoint trail No. 1441. An up-and-down traverse emerges from trees, reaches a small campsite in ½ mile, and yields to steep and steeper tread climbing to the 8243-foot summit, 9½ miles from the road.

Artifacts of the vanished lookout abound: the leveled summit, scraps of metal, and an open-air privy that may have the most spectacular view of any such facility in the Northwest.

Lake Chelan from Pyramid Mountain

94 SOUTH PYRAMID CREEK LOOP

Round trip 18 miles
Allow 2–3 days
High point 7150 feet
Elevation gain 3200 feet
Hikable July through October

Map: Green Trails No. 114
   Lucerne
Current information: Ask at
   Entiat Ranger Station about
   trail Nos. 1437, 1439, and 1433

Forest, meadows, views, choice camps, a babbling stream. What more? In early summer, flowers and love are in bloom. In late September, larches are old gold, the best kind. The loop can be done either way, of course, but to avoid climbing an extremely steep mile while wearing a heavy pack, it is described here counterclockwise. A number of delightful campsites lie along the way and solitude in this seldom used valley is almost assured.

Set out on North Fork Entiat trail No. 1437 (Hike 90), trailhead elevation 4000 feet. In 1¼ miles turn right on South Pyramid Creek trail No. 1439, whose steep sections happily are short. At about 2½ miles from the road cross the creek on a log. At a bit past 3 miles cross Butte Creek and, soon after, South Pyramid Creek—with difficulty, repeated at a recrossing in ½ mile.

At 5¼ miles from the road the South Pyramid Creek trail ends at a junction with Pyramid Mountain trail No. 1433. Keep straight ahead, proceeding up the valley. The way steepens and crosses the stream twice more, but the labors are more than adequately compensated by meadows, views, and choice camps.

At 6¾ miles pass the Pugh Ridge trail. At 7 miles cross Grouse Pass, 7150 feet. The trail drops to a crossing of Grouse Creek, 6600 feet, 8½

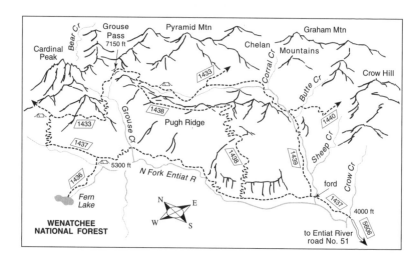

miles, traverses a steep, broad-view hillside, and at 10 miles intersects North Fork Entiat River trail No. 1437, 6600 feet (Hike 90).

If ready to camp, stay on the Pyramid Mountain trail several hundred yards to a broad meadow flat. Otherwise follow the North Fork trail steeply down (the reason for not doing the loop clockwise) to camps at 11 miles, and more at 12 miles, at the Fern Lake junction (Hike 92). The loop continues downvalley to the junction with South Pyramid Mountain Creek trail at 16¾ miles and the trailhead at 18 miles.

View near Grouse Pass

95 BUTTE CREEK–CROW HILL

Round trip 13 miles
Hiking time 2 days
High point 7366 feet
Elevation gain 3400 feet
Hikable early June to mid-October

Map: Green Trails No. 114
   Lucerne
Current information: Ask at
   Entiat Ranger Station about
   trail Nos. 1437, 1439, and 1440

This trail has two reputations: one of the very best in the Entiat valley and one of the absolute worst. Make your own judgment as you climb with scarcely a switchback beside one waterfall after another to the view from Crow Hill where you only need a springboard to do a swandive into Lake Chelan, a vertical mile below, and as you gaze to the circle of large mountains, icy mountains, naked mountains, brown mountains, and green mountains. Yet if this view is your sole goal, you can achieve it in 1 scant mile from road No. 5900 (Hike 89)—but more miles from your car than that if the road is not drivable. The serendipity here is gaining the views on a trail so steep it is legally closed to horses.

Hike North Fork Entiat trail No. 1437 (Hike 90), trailhead elevation 4000 feet, for 1¼ miles and turn right on South Pyramid Creek trail No. 1439 another 2 miles to the junction of Butte Creek trail No. 1440, 4800 feet. Because of the steepness to come, it is recommended that hikers camp at the crossing of South Pyramid Creek (the nicest place) or of Butte Creek, in order to be carrying only a day pack for the morning's ascent, 1800 feet in 2 miles.

Near the top of the first steep pitch, spot a magnificent waterfall, almost hidden in the greenery. In about ½ mile cross Butte Creek, wet your face, and resume wetting your back and brow with sweat. At about 1¼ miles the trail, still steep, comes to a ridge with the beginning of views. At about 1¾ miles it levels and tread all but disappears

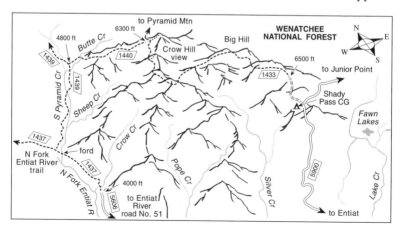

One of many falls on Butte Creek

in a short drop to a junction with Pyramid Mountain trail No. 1433, 6300 feet.

Had enough? If not, meander the short distance to the top of the 6653-foot knoll you have just passed. Great views! Not yet enough? Turn right on the Pyramid Mountain trail, steeply up to a 7000-foot high point. Where the path levels, leave it and stroll open meadows to Crow Hill, 7366 feet. Examine the remains of the ancient cabin. The terrain is so badly eroded one speculates this was a sheepherder's shelter.

96 DOMKE LAKE

Round trip 6 miles
Hiking time 3 hours
High point 2200 feet
Elevation gain 1100 feet
Hikable June through October
One day or backpack

Map: Green Trails No. 114
   Lucerne
Current information: Ask at
   Chelan Ranger Station about
   trail No. 1280

The trail gives some fine views of Lake Chelan. The lake at trail's end, Domke, has fish (and for each one, three fishermen). Children for whom no summer is complete without a swim but for whom Chelan is too refreshing find Domke sufficiently warm by mid-July for hours of splashing. Though the trip is short enough to be an easy day, families often backpack to spend a lazy week, either camping at trail's end or renting a boat to reach private sites across the lake. As for other entertainment, the odds are that one fisherman in three may get lucky.

Drive to Chelan town or Field Point on Lake Chelan and board the *Lady of the Lake.* For current schedules and fares, call the Lake Chelan Boat Company at (509) 682-2224 or the National Park Service–U.S. Forest Service Information Center in Seattle. The present pattern is daily service from late spring to early fall, dwindling to three boats a week in midwinter; the summer departure time from Chelan town is 8:30 A.M. and from Field Point 9:45 A.M., but the schedule could change. In late morning debark at Lucerne, elevation 1096 feet.

Find Domke Lake trail No. 1280 at the boat dock. The trail parallels the road to the Railroad Creek crossing then starts a dry and dusty climb of 250 feet to a great view of Lake Chelan. Forest closes in, thinning enough at about 1½ miles for more views. At about 2¼ miles is a split. The Emerald Park trail (Hike 97) goes straight ahead; turn left.

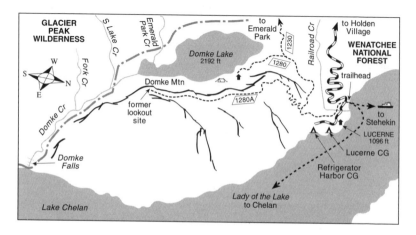

Ups and downs lead to the private concessionaire's buildings and bathing beach and rental boats at 2¾ miles. The public campground is at 3 miles, 2200 feet.

If views are the goal, at 1 mile from the Lucerne dock go left on Domke Mountain trail No. 1280A, a seldom-used 4½-mile path gaining 3000 feet to the former site of a fire lookout on the summit, 4061 feet. The building, long gone, was perched atop a 110-foot steel tower. To see the same views one must roam from side to side of the rounded mountain—rounded because the ancient Chelan Glacier rode right over the top, meanwhile gouging out the side-channel now occupied by Domke Lake.

Domke Lake

97

EMERALD PARK

Round trip 16 miles
Allow 2–3 days
High point 5404 feet
Elevation gain 4300 feet
Hikable July to October

Map: Green Trails No. 114
  Lucerne
Current information: Ask at
  Chelan Ranger Station about
  trail Nos. 1280 and 1230

The jagged giants clustered about Milham Pass—Saska, Cardinal, and Emerald, all about 8500 feet—catch the eye from afar. At the base of their cliffs is a meadow valley so richly green that when seen from a distance, such as a viewpoint in the Sawtooth Range across Lake Chelan, it seems an impossible dream. Of the many hikers who have had the vision, relatively few achieve the reality because access from one direction, the Entiat valley, is guarded by Milham Pass, 6663 feet, often plugged up with snow until mid-August, and from the other by the expense and inconvenience of travel on Lake Chelan. Though the hiking mileage from the lake makes a reasonable 2-day and easy 3-day trip, boat complications either add a day or two or keep hikers in a constant sweat worrying about connections. Lovely as the meadow is, there's not much exploring to be done unless one has the mountain competence to cope with Milham Pass.

Take the *Lady of the Lake* to Lucerne (Hike 96), elevation 1096 feet.

Hike Domke Lake trail No. 1280. At the lake junction, 2¼ miles, go straight ahead. (However, due to the midday start, you may wish to spend the first night at Domke Lake.) At about 3 miles from the dock pass the Railroad Creek trail. The way contours a steep hillside, in spots angling upward quite strenuously, gives glimpses of Domke Lake, and rounds the corner into the valley of Emerald Park Creek. The trail stays far above the water, whose sound is tantalizing as a dream on those sultry days when the flies go mad with blood lust. Openings in the forest begin and grow larger, the sun baking resins from the snowbrush, suffusing the air with the distinctive *"Ceanothus* reek."

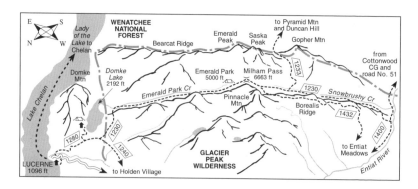

At about 6½ miles the trail levels out some and enters a meadow purple with asters, ringed by mountain ash. At 7 miles is a nice streamside camp, 5000 feet. In 1 more mile are larger meadows—the emerald gleam that so entrances the eye when seen from the high ridges across Lake Chelan.

The trail continues to 6663-foot Milham Pass, easy and safe after the snow melts, and with meadows not so jewel-lush, more of the rock-garden variety, but with big views across Lake Chelan to the Sawtooths; the drier climate here supports a distinctly smaller bug population. If a two-car switch can be arranged, or a friend recruited to do the pickup, the best way to do this country is with a one-way hike, exiting via the Entiat River trail (Hike 86).

Emerald Park from near Milham Pass

98 LYMAN LAKES

Round trip 20 miles
Allow 2–3 days
High point 6000 feet
Elevation gain 2700 feet
Hikable July through September

Map: Green Trails No. 113
   Holden
Current information: Ask at
   Chelan Ranger Station about
   trail Nos. 1256 and 1256C

Ever since Professor Lyman conducted his investigations of the glaciers at the turn of the century, the Lyman Lakes have been perhaps the single most popular spot in the Glacier Peak area. Long before any but a few had heard of Image Lake, packtrains with as many horses as the Sioux had at Little Big Horn were hauling summer-outing hordes up from Lake Chelan via Lucerne or Stehekin, or over the passes from the Entiat River and the Suiattle River. The lakes seem to be on the way to anywhere, or not far off the track. The sidetrip from the Pacific Crest Trail is short. Climbers basecamp to do the big peaks. Off-trail explorers cross the dramatic pass from Spider Meadow.

The quick (not very) access is to take the *Lady of the Lake* to Lucerne (Hike 96) and, upon debarking, pay the folks of Holden Village (an old mining town that once was the largest single customer of the Washington State Liquor Commission and now is operated by the Lutheran Church as a Christian retreat) to ride their bus to the village, elevation 3300 feet.

It will be well along into afternoon by the time you have hiked the road the 1 mile from the village to Holden Campground; the notion of spending the first night here will have some appeal, though other camps are situated at short intervals up the Railroad Creek valley. A hiker in this valley will gain the impression that a major segment of the population of Holden Village, possibly outnumbering the Lutherans, is bears.

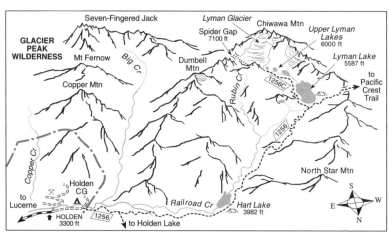

Campground deer can be just as destructive as bears.

At night hang food and toilet articles and anything with an interesting odor, shape, or color from the cables provided at Rebel Camp, Hart Lake, and Lyman Lake. Elsewhere, stand by to bang pots. However, if you camp off the beaten track, in a spot the bears don't expect to find goodies, you may sleep in peace. If you choose a crowded camp on the principle of safety in numbers, your best chance of fun will be to have a large supply of flash bulbs and spend the night taking candid photos of half-dressed campers banging pots.

At ¾ mile from the road-end campground pass the Holden Lake trail. At 3½ miles skirt Hart Lake (camp), at 4½ miles Rebel Camp (good sites), and at 7 miles reach the outlet of Lower Lyman Lake, 5587 feet (camps here and at the head of the lake).

The best is yet to come. Cross the outlet on trail No. 1256C and switchback up 500 feet, from subalpine forest and parkland into wide-open meadows. Pass the several Upper Lyman Lakes and at 10 miles from Holden come to the toe of the Lyman Glacier, 6000 feet.

The glacier has retreated from its maximum of the "Little Ice Age," as photographed by Professor Lyman, but still flows impressively from Chiwawa Mountain, 8459 feet, and is among the safest opportunities for a hiker to touch a living glacier.

The heather meadows near the middle of the Upper Lyman Lakes cannot withstand the impact of camping; set up housekeeping on the moraine near the glacier or on any bare soil 200 feet from water. Carry a stove; the wood here is too scarce and picturesque to waste in camp-fires.

99 AGNES CREEK– LYMAN LAKE LOOP

Loop trip 43 miles
Allow 3–7 days
High point 6438 feet
Elevation gain 4900 feet
Hikable mid-July through
  September

Maps: Green Trails No. 82
  Stehekin, No. 81 McGregor
  Mtn., and No. 113 Holden
Current information: Ask at
  Chelan Ranger Station about
  trail Nos. 2000 and 1256

Here's a favorite of loopers: ascending one of the supreme long-and-wild, low-to-high valleys of the North Cascades to Suiattle Pass, then climbing over Cloudy Pass and descending past Lyman Lake and Holden Village to Lake Chelan.

Hikes from Lake Chelan involve unusual transportation to and from trailheads. In this case there are the *Lady of the Lake* (Hike 96), which drops the party off at Stehekin and picks it up at Lucerne, the Park Service shuttle bus up the Stehekin road, and the Lucerne bus down from Holden Village (Hike 98). The trip plan must take into account that hikers probably won't get started on the trail until midafternoon of the first day and must be off the trail by midmorning of the last day to catch the boat.

From Stehekin Landing ride the bus 11 miles to High Bridge Ranger Station. About 500 feet beyond the bridge, on the left side of the road, is the Agnes Creek trailhead (Pacific Crest Trail No. 2000), elevation 1600 feet.

The trail drops a few feet, crosses Agnes Creek, and commences a long, easy grade in lovely forest with notable groves of cedar. Glimpses ahead of Agnes Mountain and glaciers on Dome Peak; to the rear, McGregor Mountain. A good stop the first night is Fivemile Camp, 2300 feet.

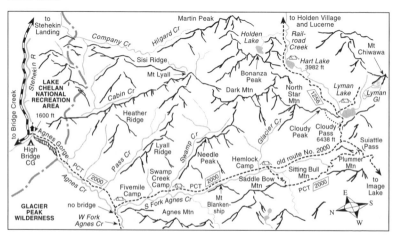

Air view of Lyman Lake, Upper Lyman Lakes, Lyman Glacier and Chiwawa Mountain

The valley forest is ever superb, featuring a fine stand of large hemlock and fir near Swamp Creek; there's another good camp here at 8 miles.

At Hemlock Camp, 12 miles, the trail splits. The new Pacific Crest Trail crosses the river, climbs to high views on the side of the valley, and at 19 miles reaches timberline campsites at a junction, 5600 feet. You can also get here via the old valley trail, which may be the better choice in early summer, when the new trail is likely to be largely in snow.

For a mandatory sidetrip, go right at the junction 6 miles to Image Lake (Hike 12), for the day or overnight.

For the loop, go left over 6438-foot Cloudy Pass to Lyman Lake and another must-do sidetrip, to Upper Lyman Lake and Upper-Upper Lyman Lake, ringed by barren moraines left by the source of icebergs, the glacier flowing from 8459-foot Mt. Chiwawa (Hike 98).

Finish the loop down Railroad Creek to Holden Village, by bus to Lucerne, and boat down Lake Chelan.

100 PACIFIC CREST TRAIL

One way from Stehekin River to
  Stevens Pass 98 miles
Allow 10–15 days
Elevation gain 17,000 feet
Hikable July through September
Maps: Green Trails No. 81
  McGregor Mtn., No. 113

Holden, No. 112 Glacier Peak,
  and No. 144 Benchmark
Current information: Ask at
  Chelan Ranger Station, Lake
  Wenatchee Ranger Station,
  and Darrington Ranger Station
  about trail No. 2000

Some of the most pleasant flower-covered meadow country and spectacular scenery of the entire Pacific Crest Trail lie in this section, which traverses the west side of Glacier Peak and walks the ridge tops south to Stevens Pass.

Take the *Lady of the Lake* (Hike 96) to Stehekin and ride the Park Service shuttle bus up the Stehekin road to High Bridge Campground.

Pacific Crest Trail on side of Kodak Peak

Climb the Agnes valley to Suiattle Pass (Hike 99). Continue to Glacier Peak Mines (Hike 14) on the slopes of Plummer Mountain and choice of sidetrips to Upper Lyman Lakes (Hike 98), Image Lake (Hike 12), or the spectacular east side Glacier Peak alternative with its road walk and difficult fords (Hike 14).

West of Glacier, the recommended alternate: Drop to the Suiattle River, climb the Vista Creek trail over ridges and down into Milk Creek (Hike 11), cross Fire Creek Pass to the White Chuck River (Hike 19), ascend the White Chuck to Red Pass, and continue via White Pass to Lower White Pass (Hike 64). **Distance from High Bridge to Lower White Pass 66 miles, elevation gain about 12,000 feet, hiking time 6 days.** The journey can be broken by trail exits to the Suiattle River road, White Chuck River road, or North Fork Sauk River road.

The remainder of the way to Stevens Pass is comparatively level, wandering along the Cascade Crest with ups and downs, frequently alternating from east side to west side, mostly through open meadows of flowers or heather. From Lower White Pass (Hike 64) the trail stays high, dipping into forest only at Indian Pass and again at Cady Pass. From Cady Pass the route contours hillsides, traversing a mixture of forest and meadows past Pear Lake (Hike 46), climbing within a few hundred feet of Grizzly Peak, and proceeding onward to Lake Janus (Hike 49), Union Gap, Lake Valhalla (Hike 48), and finally Stevens Pass. **Distance from Lower White Pass to Stevens Pass 32 miles, elevation gain 5000 feet, hiking time 4 days.**

STILL MORE HIKES IN THE GLACIER PEAK NORTH CASCADES

This volume, named after the highest mountain in the area, covers the 75 miles from the western foothills of the Cascade Mountains to the shores of Lake Chelan, and from Stevens Pass 50 miles north to Cascade Pass. The companion volumes are *50 Hikes in Mount Rainier National Park, 100 Hikes in Washington's Alpine Lakes, 100 Hikes in Washington's South Cascades and Olympics,* and *100 Hikes in Washington's North Cascades National Park Region,* which, as the name implies, reaches to the Canadian border. Another, *103 Hikes in Southwestern British Columbia,* follows the Far North Cascades over the border to their end and extends into neighboring ranges. Shorter walks than those herein are described in *Best Short Hikes in Washington's North Cascades and San Juan Islands.* The interface of lowlands and front ridges of the Cascades is treated in *Walks and Hikes in the Foothills & Lowlands Around Puget Sound.* Approaches to routes up peaks are the subject of *Cascade Alpine Guide,* a series of three volumes.

The 100 hikes have been selected to be representative of all the varied provinces of the Glacier Peak region. However, it's a big country with many other comparable trips. The preceding books describe many. Following is a sampling—some covered by the books, some not—that can be particularly recommended. The lack of detailed directions may be compensated for by greater solitude.

Cascade River
Kindy Creek: Little-used trail in a magnificent forest to Kindy Creek.

Suiattle River
Suiattle Mountain: From road No. 2640, 1 mile of unmaintained trail to Lake Tupso and the White Creek road.
Canyon Lake and Totem Pass: Flower-covered ridge 5 miles from Image Lake.
Suiattle River to Suiattle Glacier: Magnificent forests. Trail is lost beyond Chocolate Creek. From there the route is for the experienced climber only.

South Fork Stillaguamish River
Heather Lake: Very popular 2-mile hike to an alpine lake.
Lake 22: Very popular 2½-mile hike to an alpine lake.
Pinnacle Lake: 1½ miles of poor trail to beautiful lake with views.
Meadow Mountain: Tiny meadows on a wooded ridge from Tupso Lake.
Silver Gulch trail: 1½ miles on an old miners' path to open ridges.

South Fork Sauk River
76 Gulch: Unmaintained route to old mines.

Skykomish River
Mt. Stickney: Route on logging roads and through bushes to high views.
Mineral City–Silver Creek: Rich in mining history. The walk follows an abandoned mining road and trail to Silver Lake.
Howard Creek: No trail, a bushwhacking climbers' route to Spire Mountain.
Troublesome Creek: Beautiful nature walk through woods.

Wenatchee River
South Shore Lake Wenatchee: Trail is a pleasant lakeshore path.

White River
Sears Creek: Unmaintained trail on Wenatchee Ridge.
Canyon Creek: Unmaintained trail on Wenatchee Ridge.
Panther Creek: Unmaintained trail on Wenatchee Ridge.

Chiwawa River
Raging Creek: Unmaintained trail to remote meadows.
Leroy Creek: Steep trail to meadows and camps in a basin on the side of Mt. Maude, with climbers' access over the ridge to Ice Lakes.
Phelps Ridge: Trail from the Red Mountain trail over the ridge and down to the Phelps Creek trail at a point just above Leroy Creek.
Massie Lake: 6-mile trail from Chiwawa Basin up to Massie Lake and then climbing under Pass No Pass to join the Buck Creek trail.
Basalt Peak: Stiff climb to overlook Chiwawa Valley and mountains everywhere.
Alder Creek: ORV trail that was a recommended route for hikers to Mad Lake. However, the access road for hikers has been obliterated and the valley bottom trailhead would be no fun.

Entiat River
Hornet Ridge: Trail goes 6 miles to an alpine meadow.
Hardy Drive One: Abandoned trail goes 5 miles to an alpine meadow. Excellent stand of old-growth forest.
Hardy Drive Two: Abandoned trail goes 5 miles to alpine meadow.
Miners Ridge: 2-mile flower walk burned in 1994. Trail now crossed by a private logging road. Trail open to motorcycles.
Hi Yu Trail to Lost Lake: 4 miles up and down, steep at times. ORV trail to a small lake on a ridge above the upper Mad River.
Billy Creek: Trail goes 5 miles to the Tyee Ridge trail. Open to ORVs.
South Tommy: Trail goes 6 miles to the Tyee Ridge trail. Open to ORVs.
Tyee Ridge: Up-and-down ridge-top view trail 5½ miles to Boiling Springs. Open to ORVs.
Lake Creek Basin: No lakes but miles of lodgepole pine. Open to ORVs.
Devils Backbone: Spectacular ridge-top trail, partly on a bulldozed 1994 fireline and partly on real trail open to ORVs.

Lake Chelan–Stehekin River

Holden Lake: 4-mile sidetrip from Railroad Creek to a lake in a hanging valley. Views of Mary Green Glacier on Bonanza Peak.

Flat Creek: Dead-end, 3⅓-mile trail into a scenic valley under LeConte Glacier.

Devore Creek–Company Creek loop: Long valley hike with a few meadows.

USGS MAPS

The Green Trails maps listed for each trail are all most hikers need. For the benefit of those who love poring over maps, the following 7½-minute USGS maps are listed here for each trail.

1 USGS—Sonny Boy Lakes, Cascade Pass
2 USGS—Mount Higgins, Gee Point, Finney Peak (trail not on map)
3 USGS—Mount Higgins
4 USGS—Mount Higgins, Meadow Mountain
5 USGS—Whitehorse Mountain
6 USGS—Whitehorse Mountain
7 USGS—Pugh Mountain
8 USGS—Huckleberry Mountain
9 USGS—Downey Mountain
10 USGS—Downey Mountain, Dome Peak
11 USGS—Lime Mountain, Gamma Peak
12 USGS—Lime Mountain, Gamma Peak
13 USGS—Lime Mountain, Gamma Peak, Suiattle Pass, Holden
14 USGS—Lime Mountain, Gamma Peak, Suiattle Pass, Clark Mountain, Trinity, Mount David, Glacier Peak East, Glacier Peak West
15 USGS—White Chuck Mountain
16 USGS—Pugh Mountain
17 USGS—Pugh Mountain, Lime Mountain
18 USGS—Pugh Mountain, Lime Mountain, Glacier Peak West
19 USGS—Pugh Mountain, Lime Mountain, Glacier Peak West
20 USGS—Pugh Mountain, Lime Mountain, Glacier Peak West
21 USGS—Sloan Peak, Glacier Peak West
22 USGS—Sloan Peak
23 USGS—Sloan Peak, Blanca Lake, Bench Mark Mountain
24 USGS—White Chuck Mountain, Pugh Mountain
25 USGS—Sloan Peak, Bedal
26 USGS—Bedal, Sloan Peak
27 USGS—Bedal, Monte Cristo (trail not on map)
28 USGS—Monte Cristo
29 USGS—Monte Cristo, Blanca Lake
30 USGS—Meadow Mountain, Whitehorse Mountain
31 USGS—Verlot
32 USGS—Mallardy Ridge, Wallace Falls, Silverton

33 USGS—Mallardy Ridge (trail not on map)
34 USGS—Mallardy Ridge, Silverton (trails not on map)
35 USGS—Silverton, Helena Ridge
36 USGS—Bedal
37 USGS—Bedal
38 USGS—Bedal
39 USGS—Mount Stickney
40 USGS—Blanca Lake
41 USGS—Blanca Lake, Bench Mark Mountain
42 USGS—Blanca Lake, Bench Mark Mountain
43 USGS—Blanca Lake, Bench Mark Mountain
44 USGS—Barring
45 USGS—Evergreen Mountain, Captain Point
46 USGS—Captain Point, Bench Mark Mountain
47 USGS—Baring, Captain Point, Scenic, Skykomish (trails not
   on map)
48 USGS—Labyrinth Mountain
49 USGS—Labyrinth Mountain, Captain Point
50 USGS—Lake Wenatchee, Mount Howard
51 USGS—Mount Howard
52 USGS—Mount Howard
53 USGS—Mount Howard
54 USGS—Lake Wenatchee
55 USGS—Labyrinth Mountain
56 USGS—Labyrinth Mountain, Captain Point
57 USGS—Poe Mountain
58 USGS—Poe Mountain, Bench Mark Mountain, Glacier Peak East
59 USGS—Poe Mountain
60 USGS—Poe Mountain, Bench Mark Mountain, Glacier Peak East
61 USGS—Lake Wenatchee
62 USGS—Mount David, Schaffer Lake
63 USGS—Mount David
64 USGS—Mount David, Poe Mountain, Glacier Peak East, Clark
   Mountain, Glacier Peak West
65 USGS—Mount David, Clark Mountain
66 USGS—Chikamin Creek (trail not on map), Saska Peak
67 USGS—Schaefer Lake
68 USGS—Schaefer Lake, Trinity
69 USGS—Schaefer Lake, Trinity
70 USGS—Trinity, Clark Mountain
71 USGS—Trinity, Clark Mountain, Suiattle Pass
72 USGS—Trinity, Clark Mountain, Suiattle Pass
73 USGS—Trinity
74 USGS—Trinity, Suiattle Pass
75 USGS—Trinity, Suiattle Pass, Gamma Peak, Clark Mountain
76 USGS—Chikamin Creek, Silver Falls, Sugarloaf Peak
77 USGS—Sugarloaf Peak, Silver Falls
78 USGS—Silver Falls
79 USGS—Chikamin Creek, Silver Falls
80 USGS—Chikamin Creek, Lucerne

81 USGS—Silver Falls
82 USGS—Silver Falls (trail not on map)
83 USGS—Silver Falls, Chikamin Creek, Pyramid Mountain, Saska Peak (trail not on maps)
84 USGS—Pyramid Mountain, Saska Peak
85 USGS—Saska Peak
86 USGS—Saska Peak, Trinity
87 USGS—Saska Peak, Trinity
88 USGS—Saska Peak, Trinity, Pinnacle Mountain, Holden
89 USGS—Pyramid Mountain
90 USGS—Pyramid Mountain, Saska Peak
91 USGS—Pyramid Mountain, Saska Peak
92 USGS—Pyramid Mountain, Saska Peak
93 USGS—Pyramid Mountain, Saska Peak
94 USGS—Pyramid Mountain, Saska Peak
95 USGS—Pyramid Mountain
96 USGS—Lucerne
97 USGS—Lucerne, Pinnacle Mountain
98 USGS—Holden, Suiattle Pass
99 USGS—McGregor Mountain, Mount Lyall, Agnes Mountain, Suiattle Pass, Holden
100 USGS—McGregor Mountain, Mount Lyall, Suiattle Pass, Clark Mountain, Trinity, Mount David, Poe Mountain, Glacier Peak East, Bench Mark Mountain, Labyrinth Mountain, Captain Point

INDEX

Other titles you may enjoy from The Mountaineers:

The *100 Hikes in*™ Series
Best-selling mountain hiking guides with fully detailed trail descriptions, directions, maps, and photos:
  Washington's Alpine Lakes, 2d Ed., I. Spring, H. Manning, & V. Spring
  Washington's North Cascades National Park Region, 2d Ed., I. Spring & H. Manning
  Washington's South Cascades & Olympics, 2d Ed., I. Spring & H. Manning
  50 Hikes in Mount Rainier National Park, I. Spring & H. Manning
  55 Hikes in Central Washington, I. Spring & H. Manning

Hiking the Great Northwest: The 55 Greatest Trails in Washington, Oregon, Idaho, Montana, Wyoming, British Columbia, Canadian Rockies, and Northern California, I. Spring, H. Manning, & V. Spring
Guide to favorite Northwest day hikes and backpacks.

The ***Best Short Hikes in***™ Series
Popular hiking guides for those with limited time or energy. Includes distance, difficulty, directions, maps, and photos:
  Washington's North Cascades & San Juan Islands, E.M. Sterling
  Washington's South Cascades & Olympics, E.M. Sterling

Best Hikes With Children® in Western Washington & the Cascades, Volumes 1&2, Joan Burton
Part of best-selling *Best Hikes With Children* Series. Guides to day hikes and overnighters with families, including tips on hiking with kids, safety, points of interest, information on flora and fauna, and more.

Exploring Washington's Wild Areas: A Guide for Hikers, Backpackers, Climbers, X-C Skiers, & Paddlers, Marge & Ted Mueller
Guide to 55 wilderness areas with outstanding recreational opportunities. Notes on history, geology, plants, and wildlife, plus detailed sketch maps.

THE MOUNTAINEERS, founded in 1906, is a nonprofit outdoor activity and conservation club, whose mission is "to explore, study, preserve, and enjoy the natural beauty of the outdoors. . . ." Based in Seattle, Washington, the club is now the third-largest such organization in the United States, with 15,000 members and five branches throughout Washington State.

The Mountaineers sponsors both classes and year-round outdoor activities in the Pacific Northwest, which include hiking, mountain climbing, ski-touring, snowshoeing, bicycling, camping, kayaking and canoeing, nature study, sailing, and adventure travel. The club's conservation division supports environmental causes through educational activities, sponsoring legislation, and presenting informational programs. All club activities are led by skilled, experienced volunteers, who are dedicated to promoting safe and responsible enjoyment and preservation of the outdoors.

If you would like to participate in these organized outdoor activities or the club's programs, consider a membership in The Mountaineers. For information and an application, write or call The Mountaineers, Club Headquarters, 300 Third Avenue West, Seattle, Washington 98119; (206) 284-6310.

The Mountaineers Books, an active, nonprofit publishing program of the club, produces guidebooks, instructional texts, historical works, natural history guides, and works on environmental conservation. All books produced by The Mountaineers are aimed at fulfilling the club's mission.

Send or call for our catalog of more than 300 outdoor titles:

 The Mountaineers Books
1001 SW Klickitat Way, Suite 201
Seattle, WA 98134
1-800-553-4453